LETTING DOWN
MY
HAIR

LETTING DOWN MY
HAIR

By LORRIE DAVIS with Rachel Gallagher

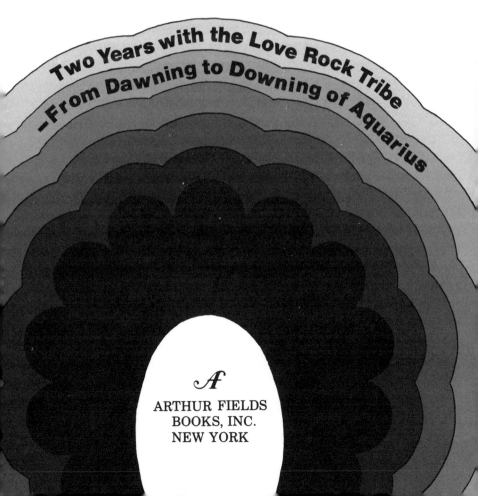

Two Years with the Love Rock Tribe
—From Dawning to Downing of Aquarius

A
ARTHUR FIELDS
BOOKS, INC.
NEW YORK

PHOTOGRAPHS BY DAGMAR FOLLOW PAGE 160

Published simultaneously in Canada by Clarke, Irwin & Company Limited, Toronto and Vancouver
ISBN: 0-525-63005-8
Library of Congress Catalog Card Number: 72-94680
Designed by The Etheredges

To Ted Landry

ACKNOWLEDGMENTS

Many people were delighted when they heard I was doing a book on *Hair,* and were very helpful in its preparation.

But I would like to give special thanks to: Erroll Addison Booker, Paul Jabara, Jonathan Kramer, Robert I. Rubinsky, Galt MacDermot, Tom O'Horgan, Nancy Potts, Julie Arenal, Michael Maurer, Charles O. Lynch, Erik Robinson, Danny Sullivan, Dennis Erdman, Didier Delaunoy, Tony Barbato, Emmeretta Marks, Jules Fisher, Eddy Williams, Warren Morrill, Sal Briglia, Marc Weiss, Neil Philips, Eddie Stover, Jill Garbar, Jean Pasteorelli, Lani Ball, Willie Weathley, Cara Robin, Harold Larkin and Carolyn and Larry Funderburk, Julie and Jerry Smaths, Norman Gladney, and Jules Fisher.

LETTING DOWN
MY
HAIR

INTRODUCTION

There was gossip in 1967 that Gerry Ragni and Jim Rado were into something very weird. It was in that year my group first performed *Futz* and the Off-Off-Broadway experience came into its full, fantastic flower. The Cafe Cino, Judson Church, and La MaMa were pumping out an endless stream of theatrical outrages. As the first decade of this century was to music, this was to the experimentation for the theater. And like horny children, eager to learn the facts of life, we ran from uncomfortable loft theaters to crowded cellar workshops to see what new theatrical ideas were to be exposed.

Jean-Claude van Itallie had just cinderized the eyes of Off-Broadway with his *America Hurrah*. He and I were working on an insane ballet for the Harkness Foundation and during a dull moment, Jean-Claude told me a curious tale about Ragni and Rado. He had heard that Gerry and Jim would choose a victim and secretly observe him for a few days, following his every move. Jean-Claude felt that he was that week's choice. In my varied rounds of the city during the next two days, I ran into Jim and Gerry seven times. I couldn't put aside the titillating thought that perhaps I was their current victim for microscopic scrutiny. Of course, I ran into Gerry regularly at Ellen Stewart's La MaMa Theater where we both were constantly involved in some project. It was there that he first mentioned *Hair* to me. "I'm writing this musical, see," he said, "and if you are interested, I'd like for you to direct it." Sight unseen, I answered, "Why not?" But when I asked him what it was about, he said, "It's a big secret." And he was right to hold on to it, because only once in a lifetime do you come upon an idea that perfectly expresses a point in time—a theater form whose demeanor, language, music, clothing, dance, and even its name accurately describe a social epoch in full explosion.

At this point, my La MaMa troupe was on its way to Europe. So, I told Gerry that when I returned I would love to work on the play. However, on returning I found the Public Theater already had Jim and Gerry's play in rehearsal. So I felt that was that. But Gerry called and asked me to come and see it; he voiced some disappointment. I was personally knocked out by it, although I felt the production was condescending and very lightweight entertainment. Gerry and Jim said that after the short run at the Public Theater it was to move to Broadway. Since then many plays have moved from Off-Broadway to Broadway but at that time it was unheard of. I nodded approval but thought the idea was pure fiction.

However, Galt MacDermot's music and the concept of the play were strong enough to perform the magic necessary to head it uptown. After a series of tedious episodes, I was chosen to direct the show. It seems foolish now, but at the time the question was, "Why should I do it?" I remember two friends, a director and a stage designer, both warning me not to get mixed up with it. They said, "Why get involved? It's been done; the critics won't even re-review it." As it happened, they were wrong.

I had been working continuously for ten years in the avant-garde theater, directing and experimenting with all the new forms of theatrical and political communication. I had come to the conclusion that communication of ideas to a small group of friends, who already understood and agreed, was pointless and that it was time to seek out a larger and essentially unconvinced audience and purposefully set out to turn their heads in another direction. The notion of taking a concept like this and perpetrating what amounted to a theatrical sit-in or demonstration in one of Broadway's sacrosanct plaster palaces was more than appealing to me.

Assembling the right cast proved to be quite a chore. Most of the original downtown cast lacked the qualities we needed. We were looking for Rock singers who were really part of the street scene of that time. We went through endless low-yield auditions. Agents would send us glossy, highly polished young singers who had no notion of what we were looking for. The problem was the people we needed not only didn't care about the Broadway theater, they didn't know it existed. Frustration was so high we had taken to chasing anyone down the street who vaguely looked right.

It was at one of these auditions that I first met Mary Davis. Besides being talented, she presented a frank, lay-it-on-the-line, slightly-angry-around-the-edges attitude that was refreshing after the long line of somewhat obsequious white-oriented black singers. Mary's directness and style were exactly what we needed to represent a truthful voice for the blacks in the show.

It's difficult to remember the naive place that Broadway was in just five years ago. Generally blacks were pictured as insultingly mild, happy for the opportunity to be with "you-all" entertainers.

New York was the first of the six productions of *Hair* that I directed. Each was a family made of young people from the community where the show was to be played.

Each cast had its own personality. New York was as different from San Francisco as Chicago was from London.
Each tribe had its share of beauty and difficulties. Like
any family it constantly grew and changed. There were
births and deaths; talents came and went; and a few true
artists emerged.

Naturally Mary's recollections in *Letting Down My
Hair* are totally different from mine. A director has the
best part of it. Working in the creation of a piece like
Hair and building the family unit that makes up the
cast is an experience that happens once in a lifetime.
Participating in six productions kept me in a state of
stoned grace for over three years. However, the director
does his work and moves on while the cast must stay
and live out his and the author's fantasy, night after
night. This may not always be pure ecstasy and after
the energy and joy inherent in this play have worn thin,
the performers must still get it up each and every night
to please the theater Gods.

No one knows better than Mary the relationship and
emotional bookkeeping backstage of the New York *Hair,*
and her book is more than a funny-sad document of those
many nights. It is an important view of an amazing social
phenomenon.

No one ever dreamed or expected the success that
came to *Hair.* Its instant communication united the young
people around the globe. Although many onlookers felt
it only sensationally exposed nudity and freedom, unfortunately for them they were the ones who could not par-
ticipate in its universal celebration of life.

TOM O'HORGAN

THE TRIBE—OPENING NIGHT
April 29, 1968

Donnie Burks
Steve Curry
Lorrie Davis
Ronnie Dyson
Sally Eaton
Leata Galloway
Steve Gamet
Walter Harris
Paul Jabara
Diane Keaton
Hiram Keller
Lynn Kellogg
Jonathan Kramer
Marjorie LiPari
Emmeretta Marks
Melba Moore
Natalie Mosco
Suzannah Norstrand
Shelly Plimpton
James Rado
Gerome Ragni
Robert I. Rubinsky
Lamont Washington

MANAGEMENT AND STAFF

BOOK & LYRICS BY: Gerome Ragni and James Rado
MUSIC BY: Galt MacDermot
EXECUTIVE PRODUCER: Bertrand Castelli
PRODUCED BY: Michael Butler
DIRECTED BY: Tom O'Horgan
DANCE DIRECTOR: Julie Arenal
COSTUMES BY: Nancy Potts
SCENERY BY: Robin Wagner
LIGHTING BY: Jules Fisher
PRODUCTION STAGE MANAGER: Fred Rheinglas
GENERAL MANAGER: Richard Osorio
STAGE MANAGER: Michael Maurer
ASSISTANT STAGE MANAGER: Donnie Burks
PRODUCTION COORDINATOR: Cara Robin
DIRECTOR OF SALES: Joe Cavallaro
COMPANY ASTROLOGER: Maria Crummaire
COMPANY CARD READER: Earl Scott
COMPANY PHOTOGRAPHER: Dagmar
RADIO AND TV RELATIONS: John Prescott
PRESS REPRESENTATIVE: Robert Ganshaw, Michael F.
Goldstein, Inc.

MUSICIANS

CONDUCTOR & ELECTRIC PIANO: Galt MacDermot
GUITAR: Steve Gillette, Alan Fontaine
BASS: Jimmy Lewis
WOODWINDS / REEDS: Zane Paul
TRUMPETS: Donald Leight, Eddy Williams
PERCUSSION: Warren Chaisson
DRUMS: Idris Muhammad

1

I am sitting in the middle of my living-room floor in one big state of confusion when the phone rings. It's a good friend of mine, Ted Landry. He tells me he has just heard that the casting people for *Hair* are looking for a black girl to replace one who has suddenly left. He says: "I told them I know just the girl they are looking for."

At that point, "Just The Girl They Are Looking For" is looking around at her newly painted apartment, wondering what to do next about getting it back into some kind of livable order. What a mess!

"I made an appointment for you to audition for them at six tonight," Ted says.

Tonight? I turn right off. I have no time to think about an audition, and the mention of *Hair* does nothing to me. About a year or so ago, in *Show Business,* I had seen the name in connection with a call for auditions for Joe Papp's Shakespeare Festival at the Public Theater. I didn't pay any attention because I thought whatever the play was, it was strictly Shakespearean and that is not my thing. Then, when *Hair* was moving uptown to the Cheetah discotheque, I auditioned for the Off-Broadway people. I never heard anything from them and assumed they had passed me by. Much later I found out they were in the midst of a management turnover, and the girl I was supposed to replace didn't leave at all but stuck with the show for its Cheetah run. I didn't know or care what *Hair* was about the first time I auditioned, and I'm not about to drop everything for a second try.

"No thanks, Ted. I don't want to go."

He is insistent. Ted is one of the most beautiful people I know. We met when I was doing a musical revue at the Falmouth Theater in Cape Cod, and he was working at the theater with management. He always expressed faith in me and my singing. "You're going to make it," he would tell me. "You should do more." He's one of the few people I would do almost anything for. I agree to go to the audition.

Hanging up the phone and glancing around my apartment, a shambles, I nearly change my mind. But a promise is a promise, especially to Ted.

I hunt around for the outfit I want to wear, an outfit I feel I look good in, especially for an audition. It is stuck in the bottom of some boxes piled in the middle of the living room. I can't find my music, a rock song called "One Two Three," which I always use for auditions, and decide to pick up another copy of it on the way to the rehearsal studio. I am frantic.

The Variety Arts, a big, gray, dusty building, gives me the feeling that this is what Broadway is all about the minute I walk in the door. Most of my ideas about the theater come from old movies, and the building looks like a set, complete to the old backstage guard at the desk who glances up at me questioningly when I walk in. I'm not sure the creaky elevator, which crawls up to the fourth floor, will make it. But it does, and the minute I step out, the old Hollywood movie instantly turns into New York reality: waiting in the hall to audition are about eight or ten of the most scruffy-looking people I ever saw. I am dressed in black walking pumps, white net stockings, a brown woolen, bulky-knit sweater dress, pearls, and white gloves. My hair is combed straight back, neat. These kids look like they have never seen a comb or a bathtub. They are slouched all over the place, dressed in uniforms of bell-bottom jeans and long, straggly hair. If they think it's "hip" to look poor, that's their thing. I can't get into it.

I give my name to some guy with a clipboard. Although he is dressed straighter than the others, he is still very casual. Every other audition I had ever been to was a suit-and-tie affair.

While I am waiting my turn, I bump into an old friend of mine from acting school, Pam Hall. She's also waiting around to audition, and when I hear that, I know it's all over. Pam and I studied musical comedy together at HB Studios. The only way to describe her singing is—fantastic. People used to applaud her in class. I don't feel I am any competition for her vocally. I have a two-octave range, she has twice as much. If it hadn't been for Ted I might have split. But I don't want to make him look bad. I knew he gave me a good build-up.

Pam is called. I can hear her singing "Going Out of My Head," and I am convinced that even though she is white, she has the part wrapped up. I just assume that a black part will go to a white if they decide she's the one they want.

Just as I am telling Pam how good she sounded, the

guy with the clipboard calls my name: "Mary Davis." (Lorrie is my stage name.)

No sense in worrying about it now, I think. How can I follow her act?

I am usually never scared at auditions, just apprehensive. The minute I see Pam all I want to do is go in, do my song, and get out as quickly as possible.

By the time I walk into Room 401 I feel very relaxed. I have nothing to lose. Clipboard announces me.

It is a large brightly lit room with wall-to-wall mirrors surrounded by ballet exercise bars. But something strange is going on here. With the exception of the piano player, and the guy with the clipboard, not one person out of a half-dozen or more is sitting on any chairs. There are upholstered folding chairs scattered all around the room, all right, but the people are sprawled on the floor. That does it for me: "I'll just do my song and get in the wind."

The next thing I see is this guy's flaming red hair; it's all over the place. He is almost grotesque. I have to laugh when I look at him. He and a long-haired, blond guy look as if they should be down on the Bowery some place. The redhead is dressed in a raggedy-red shirt, almost in tatters, and the blond fellow has on a pair of boots with very worn-down heels. The redhead seems to think I'm pretty funny, too. He is all smiles. I pick up on it and like him immediately. Good vibes. The blond seems more reserved, tense.

The next one who gets to me is the piano player. His hair is actually short, in the style of the fifties, and he has a non-stop smile on his face. The contrast between him and the others is comical. He looks like an insurance salesman.

I have been to a lot of auditions and seen a lot of

strange people, but I have never seen a weirder bunch than this. The director and choreographer are there, but I no longer care at this point. I just want to get out.

The redhead picks up on this. In spite of his ragpicker appearance, he is very handsome; there is also a wild, mischievous air about him. His eyes give him away: they are saying one thing while he's doing another. The whole thing is a big goof for him. He's falling out all over the place. On one hand I have to keep from laughing, and on the other I feel like dying. Every time I look at the blond guy's beat-up boots I wonder, "What is this? These people are trying to hire me for a job, and look at them!" Where I come from, the heels of your shoes are worn down because you can't afford otherwise.

Clipboard asks me some preliminary questions: my name, address, what I am going to sing.

I tell him and hand my music to the piano player, who still looks like someone else's second choice to me. "Play the song the way it is written, in C, please."

I don't want to hassle keys, because I'm not all that sure he can play too well. He is still smiling.

I walk back to the center of the room. The piano player starts to play, and the second I open my mouth, something is wrong. He is playing in a lower key. I can sing in that key, but I sound better in the higher one.

In acting school you're always told that once you begin an audition, you should never stop. Just go right through it until you're finished. I don't have to think twice, I call a halt to my song immediately.

"Now wait a minute. Something is wrong. Somebody's making a mistake. He's not playing in the key I'm singing in. You're gonna have to wait a minute while we get ourselves together."

The redhead falls flat on the floor with laughter over

this. They are all laughing now, but he is the loudest. The piano player never stops smiling. I am convinced there is something really wrong with all of them: "Let me get my work done and get out of here because these people ain't wrapped too tight."

After the piano player and I get the key together I sing the song straight through. After I finish, and as I'm picking up my music, I tell him: "You know, you don't play Rock music badly for a white guy." Most of the white pianists I know don't play it well.

He doesn't say a word, and I leave him the same way I found him—smiling. The others, especially the red-head, are still carrying on. I take another look around, thinking it will be my last.

It is obvious that I will never even be considered for the part after my lousy beginning and Pam's audition. Clipboard stops me on my way out. "Do you dance?" he asks.

"Yes."

"Where can I reach you later on tonight?"

I think he must be kidding. "You must be kidding." He's serious.

"You're not going to use me," I tell him, as I hand over the number of my answering service.

2

There was a jingle we used to chant as kids: "If you're white, all right. If you're brown, stick around. If you're black, get back." It was like a mindless slogan.

Growing up on the Lower East Side is different from growing up in Harlem or Bedford-Stuyvesant. It was integrated—Italians, Jews, and blacks were all living on top of one another.

We all played together as children. But as we got a little older, around the age when boys and girls start digging each other, one white friend told me her mother didn't want her to play with me anymore. I didn't understand why then, and I don't now. To separate us because of color? The experience gave me a shock of *white* recognition. For the first time, I saw why a black could be prejudiced against a white.

My mother never said anything to us one way or another about white people. It was up to us to decide.

Poverty was a common denominator but not an equalizer. There were different levels of being poor. If your parents struggled to bring home sixty dollars a week for a family of six, that was one kind of poverty; if they owned a grocery store, that was another; being on Welfare was another. We were on Welfare.

Seven of us, including my mother, lived in a four-room apartment on Pitt Street. My mother worked when she could. Welfare in itself is not degrading—what some people do with the Welfare checks is. I don't recommend Welfare for anybody. It's just another way to keep you down, and most people, especially those who think they're getting away with something, are just too dumb to see it. They're only fooling themselves.

My mother and father separated when I was still very young. They are both dead now. They moved up from the South, and something happened to their lives when they came North. Things weren't going too well between my parents even when my twin sister, Martha, and I were born. We were numbers four and five, I had an older brother, but he had been killed in a fire long ago.

My father was a gospel singer, among other things. I heard him sing a few times, but it was usually when he was high. The memory is hazy. He used to take us to the corner bar with him. He'd buy himself drinks and the bartender would give us shot glasses with a taste of whatever my father was drinking in them. To this day I don't like the taste of alcohol. I don't mind if other people want to drink, but for me it's no good. I don't like what booze can do to people, what it did to my father.

My oldest sister, Laura, has gone back to college to get her degree in nursing. So has my twin sister, Martha. I'm very proud of them both.

Martha and I, even though twins, could not be more

different. Whatever you may think of me, she's the opposite. Martha rarely gets angry. She's very even-tempered. She'd rather walk away from an argument whereas I feel challenged by one. When we were children I would try to protect her if someone got rough. It seemed to embarrass her. "Mary, if you don't stop, I'm going to tell Momma," she would say. We don't even look alike—she's shorter and a bit on the stout side. She's also married with three kids.

I was always different from my family. We're all very different in personalities and attitudes, but when it comes to our moral standards we're basically—very basically—all similar. My mother kept us straight. She brought us up to respect certain principles. There were no written rules of the house. You didn't curse, smoke, drink, or take drugs simply because my mother didn't do any of those things. The only alcohol around our house was in a bottle labeled "rubbing," and nothing stronger than aspirin was in the medicine chest. She didn't have to say a word. The vibes were strong enough: whatever it is you want to do that might displease Momma, don't.

The house was strictly for family. We could bring friends home but never for dinner or to stay overnight. It was the same at anyone else's house. My mother thought it might look like we were asking for food because we were hungry or looking for a roof because we had nowhere else to go. Or even worse, because no one cared about where we were. She was Southern, and she was proud; and pride is something no one can take away from you.

There were a lot of household mottoes, but one of the most quoted was "Never beg, borrow, steal, or lie."

Especially lie. I never did, and sometimes there'd be hell to pay, not because I told the truth, but because the truth brought out the fact that I had disobeyed Momma.

We were brought up to respect adults, absolutely, and to believe in the Bible. I don't think a day went by when I didn't hear her say, "Honor Thy Father and Thy Mother And Thy Days Shall Be Long Upon This Earth." Above all, we were taught to believe in the Ten Commandments and the Golden Rule. In her own way, my mother was very religious. The Ten Commandments and the Golden Rule held universal truths which if followed to the letter, she believed, would solve everyone's problems everywhere. I personally believe the world would be in a lot better shape if more people would abide by them, especially the part about "Do unto others . . ."

Growing up in the streets there's a lot of stuff you can get involved in, and you only do what you want to— smoking, drugs, stealing. My mother used to say, "You reap what you sow." In her own way she was telling us, "You pay dues." The unwritten laws of the household spilled out into the streets: there are certain things you don't have to experience to know that they're going to hurt you.

There was a saying: "Ain't nobody going to hang around with a junkie but another junkie, or his pusher." You *know* when you come up from the streets. It was going on all around us, but it wasn't as open as it is now.

When I first went into *Hair* I knew I was in a crazy house. Drugs and sex were easy to come by, only instead of being on the street, they were backstage in a theater, and instead of being surreptitious, they let it all hang out.

While growing up, I picked up on sex as I went along. Nobody had to teach it to me. Anyway, the subject was taboo in our house. My mother never talked about it, but she never held us back from going to parties or out on dates. Sex was just never a big thing. People were forever having babies; someone was always running off with that one's man, or woman, or whatever. Nobody ever had to tell me that sex was a *fact* of life.

My mother had high hopes for all of us. She wanted us to get more out of life than she did. She had wanted to be a teacher, but coming from the South she never had a chance. Of the six of us, only one, my sister Rita, didn't graduate from high school. My oldest sister, Laura, turned me on to nursing at first.

I took a practical nursing course when I was in high school. After that I took my state boards and got my license. I also got a scholarship to go to college nights. I went to the School of General Studies at Hunter and worked from nine to five as a staff nurse during the day.

Unfortunately I wasn't a good student because show business was in the back of my mind the whole time. It gnawed at me. But whenever I expressed my interest in it at home, all I heard from my mother was, "Get your education. You are black and you need your education." Or, simply, "You can't sing. Shut up." I spent a lot of time feeling bad, then one day I stopped feeling altogether. I just blanked it all out.

My mother and I did not get along. We did not see eye to eye. Whenever I wanted something I had to sit down to figure out a way to get it. My whole childhood seemed to be a series of getting things I did not want. For instance, I wanted singing lessons, I got dancing. But, if I could finagle something indirectly, or get my sisters and brother to ask for me, then I knew I had a better chance. It wasn't manipulation so much as knowing exactly what I could and could not have, and working my way from there.

I was lonely as a child. I spent a lot of time taking long walks, wandering around areas outside my neighborhood where there were beautiful apartment buildings. The streets were tree-lined and many of the buildings had doormen outside. When I looked at them I'd think, "That's what I want."

Or when I watched the Academy Awards on television, and someone got up to accept the Oscar, I'd say to myself, "I'm going to win one of those. I'm going to win one."

About the only real friend I had as a child was music. My sixth-grade homeroom teacher at P.S. 4 on Pitt Street, Mr. Levinsky, turned me on to classical music. We listened mostly to gospel at home. Through him I learned to dig everything from Bach to opera. With the exception of hillbilly, I loved all music.

The sixth grade put on Aaron Copeland's "Billy the Kid" that year. I wanted the lead for the ballet, but I knew I wasn't good enough. It was given to a friend of mine who had been taking dancing lessons nearly all her life. One day, I thought, I'll get my chance. But I never expected that anybody would give it to me for nothing or that there wouldn't be a lot of dues-paying.

At one point it seemed my whole life was nothing but a series of appointments for lessons—acting, singing, dancing—which never amounted to anything. The hours I spent in college should have been devoted to auditions. The pressure of taking lessons, going to college, and working as a nurse got so heavy that I nearly wore myself out. My doctor prescribed tranquilizers and ordered me to slow down. I didn't have time to think about what I was doing. I loved nursing, but it was second choice. I was willing to pay dues to get what I wanted but not destroy myself.

When I saw Carol Channing in *Hello, Dolly!* I said, "This is it, Mary. Stop fooling around with all the other shit. It's time to get it on."

I threw away the tranquilizers, switched from staff- to part-time private nursing duty, and dropped out of college. The latter was about the only "hippie" thing I ever did. I wanted to devote all my energies to the theater. I had to do what I wanted to do, or else die.

My mother's response was, "Get your education. You'll need it."

My oldest sister, Laura, said, "Do what you want to do, what you got to do." She, more than anyone else, always tried to encourage me. She seems to get a genuine kick out of what I do. Rita didn't have too much to say. Neither did Johnny or Gloria. My twin, Martha, had a similar attitude to Laura's.

I was on my own as usual.

Pam had invited me back to her place after our auditions for *Hair*. I left her number with my answering service. At about eight or nine in the evening I got a call from them saying that a Mr. Fred Rheinglas, production stage manager from the *Hair* office, had called. I couldn't believe it.

When I returned his call, Fred said, "We want you to come to rehearsals tomorrow. Be here at one P.M."

"Are you kidding? Are you really serious? You must be kidding?" was all I could say. He just laughed. Much later Fred told me that they all thought I was very funny at my audition. Hysterical, in fact.

Even though I didn't know what part I'd play in the show, or what it was about, I was up in the clouds. All I knew was that it was a Broadway show. Being in a Broadway show was all I'd always wanted and worked for.

I couldn't believe it was that easy.

3

Once again I took the temperamental old Variety Arts elevator—and walked into chaos.

By the time I joined *Hair*, rehearsals had been going on for two days. They were still auditioning, but already people were quitting or being fired from the show. As a matter of fact, they were still casting *Hair* our twenty-third day into rehearsals, fifteen days before our first public performance, and they continued to cast twelve days after we opened. They never stopped casting for *Hair*. "We didn't know what we were looking for," said Tom O'Horgan, the director, "but when we saw it, we knew we wanted it."

But on my first day—out of what was to be 755—the two-day-old cast and crew seemed like veterans of the show compared to me. I stood at the door of the rehearsal studio, looking for Fred Rheinglas, the production stage manager and the one face I knew. After wading through about twenty people, I finally found Fred, who was at the desk with a few of the production staff. He greeted me with a big, welcoming smile. He was very friendly. He showed me around, tacking names to faces, but everyone came and went in a blur. I'm not good at remembering names, only faces, but when the piano player of the day before was introduced as "Galt MacDermot, the composer of the musical score," I felt my face burn remembering what I had said to him. But Galt, too, gave me a big smile.

One of my main worries was whether I would be paid during rehearsals. If not, I would have to rearrange my work schedule—private nursing duty—around rehearsal time. When I asked Fred about it he broke up. He and some others couldn't get over it. But, "Yes," he assured me, I would be paid. I felt embarrassed over not knowing, but it seemed to be an ice-breaker.

How much I was getting paid to do the show mattered less than when. I think I would have worked for nothing during rehearsals just to be in a Broadway musical. As it turned out, I just about did. With a few exceptions, we were all getting standard minimum salary, which in 1968 amounted to $130 a week. Most of us didn't know better. We were all in the same boat: inexperienced, naive, dumb—take your pick. There wasn't one "hardened professional" or "traditional theater" person among us but, as Sally Eaton put it: ". . . everybody in the original Broadway cast was somebody fucking unique."

I didn't remember Tom O'Horgan from my audition, but as I was being introduced to him I thought he was a very up-front guy with an honest smile. Julie Arenal, the choreographer, whom I didn't remember either, looked like one of the kids. She seemed frantic.

Fred gave me some medical and publicity forms to fill out. When I finished signing my life away, he sent me out to wait for rehearsals to begin. It was one in the afternoon. I had been there about forty-five minutes already. I don't remember rehearsals ever starting on time throughout my entire twenty-five months with the show.

Our rehearsal room was one of the largest in the studio. In keeping with the rest of the place, it was big, dusty, and grayish. There were huge, shadeless windows overlooking 45th Street with a great view of Broadway's theater row. I flashed on it.

The cast was hanging around waiting to start. I stood off to the side to watch them for a while. *Who are these people?* I didn't know a soul, but one thing was certain: they were not like anybody I had ever met before. I was still apprehensive about what was going on, and what was coming next. Looking at this mixed-up group I figured anything was possible. It was too way out for me.

Melba Moore's first impression of the cast at her audition was very similar to mine. Like me she was wearing a dress, hose, and heels, and although everyone was "free acting," she thought they must have been "very poor" because of the clothes they wore. I still couldn't understand why middle-class kids were trying to run after things that I, as a black, was trying to get away from—drugs, ghettoes called "communes," etc.

People dress oddly at rehearsals everywhere, so I couldn't tell much about the kids from their clothes. It was more a matter of attitude.

I spotted the wild-looking redhead, Gerry Ragni. He was walking with a limp but acting no less extroverted. He and the more reserved blond guy, Jim Rado, the authors of the play, were standing with two other guys, one of whom I loved on sight: Steve Curry. Not only was he very sexy but he looked like a big Teddy bear. The other was Steve Gamet, who looked like Little Orphan Annie with glasses. They seemed to be a clique and acted cool and remained aloof from the rest.

Looking around, I saw a guy with a guitar. He was tall, thin, long-haired, and dressed in jeans. I thought he was a member of the cast, but he turned out to be Steve Gillette, one of the musicians in the band.

Suzannah Norstrand, a big blond, reminded me of Mae West from the way she talked and moved. I got good vibes from Diane Keaton. I liked her on sight. Natalie Mosco, who seemed a bit more "Juilliard" than the rest, and Leata Galloway, who looked Eurasian, or at least very exotic, were the first people to talk to me.

One guy seemed very nervous. That was Robert I. Rubinsky: "I felt like the oddball." I don't remember Jonathan (we called him John) Kramer that day, but he said when I arrived on the scene he thought to himself, "There's the meanest woman in town." To me John said: "When you arrived, you let it be known that you weren't going to take any shit from anybody."

People thought I was hostile when I first joined the show. In fact, they nicknamed me "Hannah Hostile." I had no idea how I appeared to them in the beginning, I was too busy picking up on them and the situation. The majority of the cast came from middle-class backgrounds, white collar. Maybe that's why I was hostile at first. I had to feel my way: it was a new street.

Finally, Julie appeared. She was in a hurry and obviously had no time to chat or horse around. You could cut with your hand the bad vibes between Julie and us.

She really looked like one of the cast, or like someone in the cast who had a little more authority than the rest. I figured she was scared. She acted like she had a job to do and she wasn't too sure about how to go about doing it.

Julie told us to form a large circle. After we were all in position, I was introduced to the cast—the attitudes suddenly had names. I felt nervous and uncertain. Nothing about this show so far was either familiar or routine.

Steve Gillette started playing one of the songs from the show, "Manchester," and Julie told us to step into a circle and she picked us at random one at a time to dance to the guitar music.

Steve Curry had to be one of the sexiest guys I'd ever met. He seemed very relaxed and languid, dancing in half-time to the rhythm. He was good. The next guy, Robert I. Rubinsky, looked like he was having convulsions on his feet. He had very little sense of rhythm and control. We all laughed; so did he. Natalie Mosco looked like a ballet dancer trying to do Rock, and Marjorie LiPari looked butch and danced more like a man than most of the boys in the cast.

Suddenly I heard my name, "Mary." I didn't know what to do and felt a split-second panic. The music was not familiar to me, and I wasn't sure of myself. Somehow I pulled through it by doing simple Rock steps.

After we all went through that number, Julie next had us imitate the person who happened to be in the center of the circle. I still couldn't figure out what was going on. Naturally, I expected to be rehearsing routines, to be taught steps. But all she did was stand around and study us. Occasionally she would throw out an order,

which we groaningly followed. She didn't seem to notice
that the cast was getting bored and restless. Nobody
understood her technique of working, and no explanations
were offered. I still had no idea of what *Hair* was all
about.

Going to Tom from Julie was like the difference
between hot and cold. Nobody seemed to understand what
Tom wanted either, but everyone went along with him
without bitching. He was firm but not tyrannical. He
rarely raised his voice. He appeared confident, as if he
knew what he was doing, and it was contagious. If he
hadn't been, I would have felt differently about going
through the paces he put us through.

When I first started rehearsing with Tom, I almost
felt like I was back in high school Phys Ed class, except
that Phys Ed was never anything like this.

He had us do what he later called "sensitivity exercises." He asked the entire cast to form four or five small
circles. That day everyone just sort of fell into clumps,
but after a few weeks cliques formed and certain people
sought each other out. Once we were in position, Tom
chose someone to stand in the center of his circle, or someone was chosen by the cast, or someone volunteered. Steve
Curry was usually an eager beaver, and Sally Eaton was
an exhibitionist. She had very little qualms about doing
anything.

Next Tom would ask the one in the center to close
his or her eyes, stiffen the body, and free-fall at random.
Those of us on the periphery of the circle were supposed
to catch him before he hit the ground and push him
upright. Once upright, the person would fall again. It
became a constant scramble to keep whoever was in the
center from falling flat on his face. We did this for about

one minute until the free-faller changed places with someone else and everyone got a chance to do it.

I wasn't crazy about the exercise. There was never much touching among members of my own family, let alone among a bunch of strangers, but I free-fell when it was my turn.

Next Tom asked us to lie down on the floor. We were going to do breathing exercises. First he asked us to pant. Then to relax and breathe normally. Next to hold our breaths then exhale slowly. I felt very uncomfortable lying on the floor doing this. I felt overexposed and vulnerable, not to mention ridiculous. These exercises were completely new to me. I couldn't figure out what they had to do with the show.

After the breathing exercises, Tom told us to remain on the floor but to concentrate on relaxing from head to toe. I really had to think hard about it. I couldn't help feeling suspicious. Tom told us that if we felt tense in a certain place, to concentrate on that spot. At that point I was concentrating on my entire body.

Then he told us to close our eyes, because it is easier to concentrate with our eyes closed. There was no way I was going to close my eyes that day. While we were doing this exercise, Tom walked around us quickly, lifting a leg here or an arm there to see if there was any tension. If we were not totally relaxed, he would coax us in a soft-spoken voice, easing us along. Sometimes we would do the exercise sitting in a chair or standing up. While standing we tried to maintain only enough body tension to keep from falling.

In the midst of all this, the producer, Michael Butler, appeared. Two things struck me about him immediately: he was tall and he seemed uptight. Fred Rheinglas introduced me to him as a new member of the cast. He didn't look me straight in the eyes, which to me always indicates a sign of insecurity. Then he said something to Fred and left. Somehow, he, as the producer, should have made it all seem official, I wasn't just imagining everything. But, still, nothing was very clear.

We were given a five-minute break. I talked to Natalie Mosco about how strange I thought the rehearsals were so far, and she said it had been that way from the start.

Toward the end of the day we met with Galt. Here was one area, finally, where I didn't feel uncomfortable. Singing was something I knew about, and out of all the directors so far, Galt was the most easy-going.

He obviously knew what he wanted as far as the sound of the show was concerned. He wanted a natural-sounding singer, not a typical Broadway-musical type. And, for the most part, that's what he had to work with. About three-quarters of the cast, including myself, couldn't read music.

Most of the parts had been assigned before I came into the show. I was given a script eventually, but the play was broken down scene by scene, as we went along. Nobody told me what I'd be doing exactly until Melba, who had joined the show a few days after I did, started singing "White Boys." For the time being, Galt sat us according to vocal sections: alto, bass, tenor, and soprano. You knew what you would sing according to where you sat. I was alto. That, apparently, was all I needed to know for the first day.

I was given a copy of the Off-Broadway *Hair* album to take home. After I heard the entire album, I understood why nothing was explained to me about the show. The music said it all. I couldn't believe how beautiful it was. I kept playing the record over and over again. I sat in the midst of all the paint cans in my apartment and turned the record player on full volume. I was falling hopelessly in love with the score. When friends called to ask how it went, I'd say, "Listen to this" or "Listen to that."

I stayed up half the night listening to that record. After a while I just replayed my favorite parts— "Starshine," "Aquarius," "Be-In." The music made me do something I never do—fantasize. *Hair* was going to be a great show, more than that, a theatrical triumph, the greatest thing ever to hit Broadway.

I found the rhythm, beat, and tempo irresistible. I didn't know it then, but Galt had lived and studied in South Africa as a boy. He was greatly influenced by African music.

Galt, a Canadian, had borrowed an African sound to compose an "American Tribal Love-Rock Musical." The "tribal love" part of the "Rock musical" was something I didn't know too much about for the time being, but the music was something else. It really turned me on.

4

The overall framework for *Hair,* I soon discovered, was "hang loose." Every department seemed to do its own thing in its own way, and some were more together than others.

One of the paradoxes of *Hair* was that we thought we were given a lot of freedom in the show when actually we were under a more rigorous regime than most Broadway productions. We were not merely doing a job, we were spreading *the Word.*

Hair was the only Broadway show that had a company astrologer and a card reader. I never saw our astrologer, Maria Elise Crummaire, she was a mystery woman to me, but supposedly she was the one who set all the *Hair* opening dates, with one or two exceptions. Earl Scott, our card reader, used to hang around a lot. He ran errands for Gerry and Jim and also read tarot cards for the cast. He read my cards and told me I was going to be a big success in the play. He also told Tom that he would become *Hair*'s director, although a few others were under consideration for the job at the time.

Early in the show Michael Butler sent around a guy from the production staff to ask everyone's birth date. Management wanted to do a chart on us. I said I didn't want any chart on me. The guy looked and sounded as though he'd lose his job if he didn't get my birth date. I was asked for my birth date on three separate occasions, and each time I gave the same day and month but a different year.

I can't take too much of that stuff seriously, but our producer, Michael Butler, was really into it. He also had a thing about American Indians. "Natoma," which was the name of both his home in Oak Brook, Illinois, and his production company, was an old Indian name. Tribes of Potawatomis and Miamis once used the multi-million dollar, 3,600-acre Butler/Oak Brook estate as their hunting grounds. I guess Michael Butler never got over the association.

Originally, his involvement with *Hair* came about by accident. He saw an ad for *Hair* which depicted people wearing beads and feathered headbands. Thinking it was a play about American Indians, he went to see it at the Shakespeare Public Theater and fell in love with it, even though it had nothing to do with Indians. For him it was a lucky, and even mystical, mistake. The rest is history.

Although *Hair* had always been billed as the "American Love-Rock Tribe," the idea that we really were a tribe started with the Broadway show. As far back as Variety Arts rehearsals we were told by Michael Butler that we were more than a cast, we were a "tribe," and that we should consider him the "chief" of the tribe. He would often come to rehearsals with some of his cronies to watch us. Sometimes he said nothing, other times he would just start talking to us after a rehearsal break. The gist was always the same: we had to work together to make the show work, and we had to come together as a tribe, like the Indians.

Tom O'Horgan was mostly responsible for the "love" aspect. He was into the hippie love thing and thought it very important to the show how we felt toward each other. He never lectured us about it, but all the rehearsals and exercises were geared to this. As the cast got more and more into the exercises and the show, they got more and more into each other and what Michael Butler, our "tribal chief," was preaching.

After we opened, the stage manager would announce when the chief wanted to talk to us. Then, flanked by his cronies, Michael Butler would come in and sit on the edge of the stage while the cast sat scattered in the audience. He would lecture us about the show and what we were doing, often in terms of society in general. Everything he said implied an attitude of "down with the Establishment" or "down with the theater Establishment." It became a kind of litany. He would tell us that rules are meant to be broken; no one should have to do anything he doesn't want to do; we are all equal; and, above all, a love-tribe, so love, love, love yourselves, one another and above all, the audience. "Loving" the audience was even part of our opening act; the cast scattered all over the theater, greeting people with flowers or body language as they filtered into the theater. Management wanted us to genuinely *love* both onstage and off. Anything less would not have the same effect on the cast or the audience. We had to be evangelical, because *Hair* set out to change people, not just entertain them.

Our tribal chief seemed to think of himself as a bridge between the Establishment and the Movement. He was the aristocrat and we were the hippies—children of the streets—all meeting on the common ground of the hippie button commandment: Make Love, Not War.

One of the girls who had been with the Off-Broadway show said, "Michael Butler thinks that *Hair* is like the start of a new civilization."

Or the " . . . flowering of a new society."* A couple of people in management told me that he really believed in and was sincere about the tribal love thing in the beginning. He even wanted to extend it into a communal powwow, where everyone would live together in peace and love. A lot of the kids went for it right away. I didn't know what to make of the "tribal" business at first.

---

*"A Weekend With Chief Michael Butler and His Inner Tribe," by Helen Lawrenson, *Esquire*, Nov., 1970

5

Tom O'Horgan wanted to take the tribal concept a step further. Ideally he thought we should actually live in the theater. He wanted to create a total environment so that when the audience walked in, they entered a whole new world. Michael Butler gave Tom freedom to do pretty much as he pleased, but covering the theater walls with psychedelic murals, living there, and throwing garbage in the aisles was out.

Tom often referred to his directing style as "kinetic sculpture." He wanted everything, all the components of the show, to flow into one single action, almost like a movie. What he did in *Hair* has been called everything from a "monumental ego-trip" to "genius."

"Esalen would take ideas and devote them to therapy for people," he said. "I was using the same emotions, but for the theater. It's all basically the same kind of communication.

"Creation is a moment of insanity. When we were building *Hair,* we just didn't know what we were getting into."

Neither did anybody else. "I felt so stiff and outside," Melba Moore said about early rehearsals. "Exposing myself to perfect strangers was really a trip for me. For me, it was therapy."

The first "trick" out of Tom's "bag" was to get us into a state of trusting each other, and him. Trust was our first exercise.

I had a lot of trouble with the trust exercises. There was one in particular which I only did once as the principle, and then only because Tom insisted. All other times he didn't. Few people ever flatly refused to do something for Tom, but in this case I felt uneasy.

The exercise involved being lifted above the heads of the cast and passed around, sometimes fast, sometimes slow, being all shook up all the while by the cast. Tom divided everyone into two groups and either asked someone to be "it" or asked for volunteers. My dread of this exercise wasn't purely distrust: I'm very uneasy in high places. On the other hand, I don't dig the idea of anybody, no matter how strong they are or how much I trust them, holding me in the air.

At first, because I didn't know anyone too well, I felt all the touch exercises were like an invasion of privacy. I wasn't alone either. "I didn't want those people touching my body," Jonathan Kramer said. Another guy who joined the show after it opened thought they were set up to "break the performer down psychologically."

The exercises varied from day to day, and after a while I got caught up in them. The more I got into them, the freer I became.

For one exercise, Tom would tell us to form a large

circle. Then, unless a person volunteered, which often happened, Tom—or whoever was conducting the rehearsal—would choose someone to stand in the center. Tom told that person to do anything he wanted and we were all supposed to imitate him. Everything was tried: body or facial contortions; jumping up and down, either stiffly or loosely; walking on our knees; crawling; calisthenics; performing turns, spins, leaps, or jumps; or doing Frankenstein or Wolfman takes. We all took turns.

Another exercise was similar except that it had sound effects. We set up in a large circle with a volunteer, and Tom would instruct whoever was "it" to make a sound to accompany a movement. After a minute, the volunteer would walk up to someone else who was supposed to pick up the same sound and movement, slowly changing it to something of his own. Most of the movements were repeats of the regular imitation exercises, but the sounds varied: humming; screaming; whispering; musical notes; different types of breathing; deep or short breaths or both; panting, gasping, or expelling air at different rates of speed; growling; groaning; whistling; and Bronx cheers. Usually everyone had a turn.

Both of these miming exercises were supposed to help us move, talk, sing, dance, and act from any position and from anywhere in the theater.

We did exercises to prepare us for the opening number of the show, a ritualistic slow motion in which the cast—scattered all over the audience—converged on the stage.

We practiced almost every kind of commonplace movement in slow motion: walking and running across the room; moving our arms, legs, hips, heads, or eyes; examining parts of our bodies or someone else's, such as arms, hands, faces; examining articles of clothing, strands of hair, fingernails; falling to the floor, standing, sitting, and different body contortions. I could always feel my muscles toning up during these exercises.

Moving in slow motion was easiest when I concentrated on my torso. It probably stemmed from my dance training. For example, when I walk or run regularly, my chest goes first, thrusting forward, then the rest of my torso follows, my legs last. Walking and running in slow motion made me very conscious of the mechanics of my body movements.

When we examined something in slow motion, the idea was the same: become absorbed by it. For example, when examining our own or someone else's hand, we were told to concentrate on looking at the color, lines, condition, beauty, or ugliness of the hand; to look for callouses, scars, or marks; to notice the condition of the nails—were they clean, dirty, short, long, bitten, filed, polished, unpolished, with or without half-moons? Were the fingers long, short, fat, skinny, or tapered? Then we were told to do the same when we felt the hand, except that another sense—touch—now came into play. We would look at and feel the texture of the hand at the same time, in slow motion. The exercise becomes very sensual if you are completely relaxed, especially when examining someone else's hand or face.

In another exercise, Tom would send someone out of the room. Then we would all decide what would be done to him when he returned. The principal, now blindfolded, would be led back to the group and be put through any number of paces. He might be lifted above our heads and passed around from person to person, then suddenly dropped to within a fraction of an inch of the floor; he might be put "Through the Mill" or dragged between our legs while we touched and tickled him. Sometimes we would put him in a dark closet, leaving him there until he was told to remove his blindfold. Other times everyone in the room would become absolutely silent for a moment, then begin to make noises which would build slowly until the pitch was nearly deafening. Then we would reverse it, slowly lowering the pitch until it faded into silence. In the meantime, everyone would quietly leave the room while the blindfolded subject was told to try to grab someone. After a few minutes of clutching at air in an empty room, he was told to remove his blindfold. He would find himself completely alone.

There were a hundred variations of this particular exercise. No one ever knew what to expect. I only took part in this one as a group member, never a principal. If I didn't like the idea of being lifted above everyone's head with my eyes wide open, there was no way I would do it blindfolded. I wasn't about to take the chance.

Other fairly standard exercises included handstands, headstands, crawling, lying on your abdomen and pulling the weight of your body with your hands and stretching to try to touch the ceiling with your fingertips. One not-so-standard exercise was trying to *feel* the space around you.

In one I really dug, Tom would ask us to act out a position in which we would least like to be caught. Everyone was always at their least inhibited and their most hammy for this exercise. We always laughed our way through it.

I would stand with my hands on my hips and say, "O.K. You're right and I'm wrong," repeatedly, with as many variations as possible. Someone else would stick his finger in his nose and then suck it; another would simulate sitting on a toilet bowl; another would pull down his pants, flash his ass, and make a fart-like sound; another would unzip his fly. One girl pulled her dress over her head. The improvisations were endless.

For another exercise, we were told to lie down on the floor on our sides. We were all lined up so that we were touching each other like bookends in a row across the floor. Then we were told to take our free hand and run it down the side of the body of whoever was in front of us. Some of the sensory exercises got even more sensual after the show opened. You could say they got hairier.

The exercises continued long after the show was a big Broadway hit.

One of the freakiest I remember took place long after we opened. Tom told us to pick out a principal from the cast. Almost simultaneously everyone looked at one particular girl. She was "it."

We were all sent to the back of the theater and told to wait there until the lights were turned out and then to proceed to the stage, individually, and do whatever we felt like doing to the principal. With the exception of a small work-light onstage, it was dark and hard to see. Somewhere in the theater someone was drumming rhythmically on a hard surface.

I was one of the last to approach the stage, and when I did, what I saw stunned me. This girl was standing totally naked, spread-eagled, with her arms and legs tied between two poles. Approaching her, I just brushed her cheek lightly with my hand, then walked off quickly. All I could think was: "That could have been me up there."

Afterwards Tom asked me why I didn't touch her

more. "Because I felt sorry for her," I said. Although I could only imagine what some of the others did to her, she didn't seem to mind the ordeal.

There was another outstanding exercise incident I remember. Tom picked out a girl in the cast and asked her to lie down, fully clothed, onstage. The theater lights were out and the stage lights dimmed. Ten or twelve cast members were chosen by Tom to touch and examine one particular part of her body. The emphasis was on "loving" and "caressing" it. He kept telling us to really concentrate; to really get into it.

I worked on her lower left leg, others on the rest of her body—legs, arms, hands, face, neck. We all touched her simultaneously, silently. The atmosphere was intense. Suddenly, she started crying, softly at first, then nearly hysterically.

I was surprised. Everybody stopped immediately and Tom called a break. Later on I asked her what had happened. She didn't want to talk about it. Although I hadn't noticed it, evidently, some people were getting into areas much more sensual than knees and elbows. This was the only time I ever saw a reaction like that to one of Tom's exercises.

Tom made rehearsals so much fun that most of us never knew how the show was put together. I had no idea of what *Hair* was about until opening night.

6

Working with Galt MacDermot was a joy. He was like everybody's favorite high-school music teacher. We had to learn twenty-nine songs, ten more than the original Off-Broadway version (although some from Off-Broadway had been dropped). As our cue to start, Galt would pound the key on the piano and we would pick up on it. He would let us invent as we went along, but he never allowed us to wander too far from the melody or change any of the lyrics. Whoever sang a solo felt free to try new things. If it didn't work, Galt would quietly suggest new ways to improve or change it.

The first time I heard Ronnie Dyson sing "Aquarius" at rehearsals I was so touched I nearly cried, and I don't cry easily. The combination of the song, his voice, and Steve Gillette's accompaniment—"Aquarius" was Steve's special thing—was overwhelming. But Ronnie could do that with almost any song.

Tom O'Horgan told me that Ronnie's audition was such an incredible experience that he wanted to put the whole thing into the show.

One day (as Tom recalls it) in the middle of a long, arduous round of auditioning—"If I heard 'Going Out of My Head' one more time, I was going to throw up."—a white, funky fifties-type jazz musician walked in with a young black boy wearing horn-rimmed glasses. The boy looked about twelve years old. Everyone looked at each other.

When the old guy sat down at the piano, it was obvious that he could play. He played in the strict tradition of fifties' jazz. It was good, but not Rock. Then Ronnie started singing.

"A certain nostalgia crept over me," Tom said. "I like Rock, but sitting there in the Old Variety Arts hearing 'I'll Never Stop Loving You' being played on that beat-up piano was almost too much. Tears came to my eyes. I couldn't believe what I was seeing and hearing. I looked around—everyone else was reacting the same way.

"It was more than just the boy singing beautifully. It was the white, funky jazz musician with a black child; one from one generation, the other from another. I think the idea for 'What A Piece Of Work Is Man' came from Ronnie's audition."

I knew what Tom meant. When I heard Ronnie and Walter Harris, who were under eighteen, sing "What A Piece Of Work Is Man," I was even further amazed by Ronnie's voice. He reached what I thought had to be his vocal peak, then hit another still higher note right after it. Sometimes I think his tenor range won't quit.

Galt had a way of making us feel like we were creating while we worked with him. He loved his music, and he knew we loved it, and we all worked together without any hassles. Some cast members told me they thought

Galt was ripping us off a little musically by adapting our interpretations for himself. But most felt the way Melba put it: "I dug the way Galt was working, because he was getting the creative things out of people, and it wasn't a studio situation."

Throughout all our rehearsals, Galt got really angry only once; he actually raised his voice. Some of the kids were cutting up while he was trying to explain something.

"Dammit!" he said.

You could hear a pin drop. We all stopped to look at him, and he broke out into a big grin. His outburst was so rare we all made a joke out of it, including him. Galt was highly respected, something which was practically unheard of around *Hair*. With nearly everyone else we were like a "tribe" of wild Indians, but when we worked with Galt we would discipline each other, tone down the noise and pay attention.

Sometimes he seemed like the only sane person in the show. "I have some areas where I'm insane," he once told me, "but they're not visible. Areas of music."

Galt never got involved with the rest of the things going down in the show. He just did his thing—he taught us his music.

Working with the dance department was a bring-down from the high we got from Tom's biogenetic fun and games or the music. It was usually chaotic.

Like Tom and Galt, Julie Arenal deliberately looked for amateurs. She didn't want anybody who was hung up on technique, and with the exception of four or five, including Natalie Mosco, whom we nicknamed "After Twelve Years of Professional Training," that's exactly what she got. All the dance movements were supposed to "evolve from the situation," but none of us were too sure what the situation was, exactly.

Julie, too, had her stock of exercises. "If you had one chance to be remembered in the world, what pose would you take?" she'd ask, and everybody would give her some crazy thing—a caricature of Napoleon or a hooker or something scatological—and she'd make use of it.

Everyone seemed to be "borrowing" ideas or interpretations. Jonathan Kramer, for one, thought Julie "got the biggest shaft in the show." In his opinion, "She used to whisper suggestions and ideas in Tom's ear and they came out of his mouth."

Julie often seemed to forget that we were *not* professional dancers. She would show us what she wanted us to do, then we'd try to imitate her. "You're a clutz," she'd tell Jonathan Kramer. "You can't dance." Or, if she didn't like the way something was done, she'd yell, "No, no, no," frantically.

"They couldn't understand this maniac," Julie said Jonathan Kramer later told her the cast was saying.

One day Julie brought in a discotheque dancer, Murray from the Cheetah, to work with us. He was good. He'd show us dance steps and movements while she just watched. Then she would take some of the steps, put them together, and try to use the "dynamic" of it: "You can't have people waving their hands all the time. . . . Sheer energy doesn't make a show."

But from one day to the next during our pre-opening rehearsals, Julie either seemed to forget what she had told us to do or would make changes without informing us. When we tried to show her what we had learned the day before, she'd get angry: "I can't use that!" she'd say, "even though I liked it." She later told me: "You were led to believe you could just go wild."

When Julie yelled it was hard to respect her or take her seriously—she was as young as we were—especially in contrast to the daddy-director moods evoked by Tom and Galt. Julie's delivery particularly rubbed most of the kids the wrong way. Like Tom and Galt, she coordinated everybody's talent, used everybody's own particular thing; but her way of going about it was nearly the complete opposite of theirs. They were soft-spoken and never seemed to insist on anything; Julie would make demands and raise her voice. She couldn't believe it if we balked, but we weren't used to such treatment.

Julie and Tom had similar ideas but different approaches. One reviewer commented that, ". . . it would take more than a single viewing . . . to know where director Tom O'Horgan left off and Julie Arenal came in." * That's right on with respect to technique, but discipline was something else.

They both talked to me about it on two separate occasions, and how each one felt is clear from their different versions:

JULIE: You all felt you could do anything you wanted. I was saying, "No, you can't . . . I want you to do it just this way."

TOM: I feel the hardest thing for most people to do is take responsibility without putting on an SS uniform and saying, "You will do this!" or "You will do that!," which is the traditional director's view.

JULIE: There is a way of demanding you do things

* Doris Hering, *Dance*, July, 1968

at certain times, getting you concentrated, and doing it in such a way that it still looks spontaneous.

TOM: I'm not saying my will isn't inflicted on the cast. Obviously, it is.

JULIE: Everyone thought that you couldn't get love and have discipline at the same time. I think you can. I was authoritarian. . . willing to take a chance that people wouldn't like me. I blanked it out.

TOM: The game, of course, is to arrange a way where the cast members have a feeling of participation and creation during the rehearsal and performance.

JULIE: No one else was demanding that you learn something—that you learn a skill. They were pretending that you just be yourself. I never pretended that.

TOM: It's more like preparing a team for a game . . .

JULIE: They (the cast) thought I was just criticizing them. I had to withstand the hostility that came from that.

TOM: When you get right down to it, very few people want freedom. They want all the trappings, but none of the responsibility of having to make something happen.

JULIE: The only way I'm really going to help you is by saying, "It is not right, and I'll tell you why. But for that moment you are going to hate me."

And we did. People got attitudes over working with Julie. All it did was waste more time. The more uptight we became, the more uptight she became. When I realized how frantic Julie was, I stopped leaning on her so hard. She was under a lot of pressure; I wasn't helping by pointing out her changes. Sooner or later you sense when someone else is the underdog.

"I was petrified in the beginning. I was only aware of getting the job done," Julie said. Much later she told me the music threw her at first: "I was brought up on long-hair."

I don't remember going through a day when the entire dance rehearsal went smoothly. We'd hop, skip, and jump one way one day, and jump, skip, and hop another way the next. Or we would shimmy and shake. There was not one full-scale dance number in *Hair,* but the show didn't stop moving for a minute. Don't ask me why.

7

By the middle of our second week of rehearsals we were at loose ends: we were cramped for space and needed another rehearsal hall; we still didn't have a theater; script revision was getting underway; and eight people were late for the first day of an early-morning call. All the guys in the show were instructed to let their hair grow down to their ankles.

Meanwhile, a few doors away from the theater that we didn't yet have, Michael Butler was assuring the League of New York Theaters that he could meet their conditions to open (for one night with a paid performance) at a legitimate first-class theater with a printed program in five days, March 19. This was to make us eligible for the Tony Awards whose new cut-off date had been moved up to March 19 from April 11. Originally, *Hair* was scheduled to open April 3.

The next day the New York Theater League turned down *Hair*'s eligibility on the grounds that it could not qualify because it was originally an Off-Broadway show. Michael Butler sued and got a temporary court injunction so that he could still qualify for the 1968 Tony's, but the case was rejected by the court.

Nobody told us why we had to leave the Variety Arts for the Ukrainian Hall rehearsal studios, we just made the shift. The location (8th Street and Second Avenue), although untheatrical, was friendlier. Uptown we were always gawked at; down there we weren't the only freaks on the streets.

Michael Butler began holding a number of "auditions" for theater owners. We were always briefed when they could be expected, and Michael Butler was polite and business-like when he spoke to us. He even dressed conservatively. We might have been better off had it stayed that way. On theater-owners' days, we usually performed the dance part of the Be-In, which was supposed to be a festival or happening, or Shelly Plimpton sang "Frank Mills."

One day the platforms, the actual stage, were brought in, and we began to realize we weren't just horsing around, we were really going to do a Broadway musical. That same day, we ran through the show from the opening to Kama Sutra, a scene at the end of Act I, for Michael Butler and the Biltmore Theater owners.

"We had great difficulty finding a theater," someone in management told me. "So when the theater contract was negotiated, it was done in favor of the theater. Their [the Biltmore's] weekly gross is higher than most shows."

The next day the Biltmore Theater was officially ours.

Since it was not a musical theater and was not technically equipped for a large musical, we could not rehearse there until the scenic and lighting designers had set up all the specialized lighting and electrical equipment *Hair* required.

The scenery and lighting were about the only things that ever remained constant in the show. Jules Fisher, the lighting designer, said that he could make no sense out of the play from reading it and didn't get excited about *Hair* until he saw it in rehearsal.

No one told him what would be needed at first. "Normally, you sit down with the director, scenic designer, and costume designer to discuss what everybody wants. The script is closely followed," Jules said. But, of course, *Hair* was different from any traditional Broadway musical, and Jules was encouraged to "extemporize outside of the script," which did not call for specific realistic detail. He mapped out his plans on paper. "We had four days to put in the lights and scenery."

Hair may have looked like a "psychedelic light show," but it was a very complex and "calculated theatrical lighting project." It required a lot of specialized custom-made material, such as strobe and blinking lights, a light which was synchronized with the music in the "Walking In Space" sequence, a rotation light for the fake police raid at the end of Act II. "It was the structure of the lighting which made it seem unstructured," Jules said.

The schedule for costume fittings was posted at Ukrainian Hall. What kind of costumes could be designed for this show? *Hair* was about street kids who hung around St. Marks Place in the East Village dressed in Army-and-Navy-store drag.

The leads were first to get fittings at the A.P.A. Theater shop. They came back with some beautiful stuff, antique clothing mostly. When I went, they just took my measurements; nobody showed me anything special, and I figured I had missed out on the good things and got upset. Then we were told that except for special costumes, the cast could select whatever they wanted from what they were given, as long as they stuck to basic pants and tops.

Despite the general belief that all clothes were dirty street rags, with few exceptions they were either sprayed or dyed to look that way. We had dressers who regularly laundered and cared for the costumes. The fact that we could wear our costumes on or off the stage was something else. Some of the kids wore the same thing every performance. I liked variety: clothes that either covered me up completely or clothes that showed a lot of skin, like hip-huggers and stretch halter tops. We were free to experiment.

"*Hair,*" said Nancy Potts, the costume designer, "was not like any other show I had ever worked on . . . I had the old Broadway rule book in mind. Tom O'Horgan said, 'Forget about the book.' But he wouldn't commit himself further. 'Just figure out a basic costume for everyone.' He left everything very loose and open."

Nancy took Tom's advice. She threw away the "book." Part of her genius was that she treated everyone in the cast specially. Each of us was given costumes he or she personally dug. It took Nancy and her staff three weeks, working day and night, to dress the show. "We did a lot of scouting. Some things were made, others came from the old costume houses." A lot, including jewelry, came from Nancy's personal antique collection, like the lush velvet jacket I wore for my role as Abe Lincoln.

Nancy tried to use her costumes to characterize certain roles. For instance, Claude, a middle-class white boy about to be drafted, was mystical. "Jim Rado expressed that beautifully. I'd say three-quarters of the cast have good freak taste." For Berger, Claude's friend who was rebelling against the Establishment, Gerry Ragni had a choice of things to wear. "His taste is infallible in the weirdest way." What *Hair* did to the fashion industry is history: it put bluejeans on the Establishment.

One person from management allegedly had second thoughts about the costuming. He was worried that the girls in the show would not be sexy enough, that the audience would be turned off by a bunch of dirty hippies with long hair, instead of the usual candy-ass chorus girls and boys.

Often when I wasn't into doing the show, just putting on the costume would get me into the mood, especially for the Be-In. (Later, taking it off for the Be-In became more important than putting it on.) In the beginning I wore a long, flower-print dress tied at the shoulder and slit up the side. Later I wore gold and purple velvet pants with a see-through gold-net top. Off stage, for an audience participation number—I didn't think they were ready to deal with it close-up—I'd cover up the see-through top. Most of the time the audience acted like they were viewing the play through a peep hole.

When Tom mentioned that a nude scene was planned for the show, most of the cast thought that was going too far. It seemed so impossible that I didn't even think about it at first.

Tom's idea was for everyone to strip during one scene. The only problem was how to go about it. Nancy Potts said they discussed faking it with body stockings, but she advised Tom to make it all or nothing. They said no more about it, but as the performance approached Tom asked if she could get a bunch of body stockings for the girls and briefs for the guys. Nancy insisted it was all wrong, and he finally agreed with her. He told her that he had "three guys who were ready and willing to strip."

Although the whole cast in general, and some of the cast in particular, was asked to strip, the nude scene was never pushed. In fact, Nancy forgot all about it during the hectic dress rehearsals, but neither Tom nor management did. Michael Butler talked to us, saying that nudity was an important part of the hippie movement; it was part of showing that you were free, liberated, together. In other words, that we were really all the things the show said we were supposed to be. Ninety-five percent of the cast felt they were being romanced for some unknown reason and had no intention of taking their clothes off onstage. Yet we all knew exactly when and where the scene was supposed to take place—during the Be-In at the end of Act I.

After chanting "Hare Krishna" and burning draft cards, the cast lies down on stage, covered by a scrim, a net curtain. Meanwhile, Claude, who's been drafted, sings his solo, "Where Do I Go?," standing fully clothed in the middle of the billowing scrim. At the end of the song, those who had stripped underneath the scrim, stand up, nude, singing "Beads, Flowers, Freedom, Happiness."

As I said, I felt the costume was very important to this scene. A certain feeling had to be evoked: this was a celebration of body and self, a plea for all of us, including the audience, to get it together. Everything about Be-In, particularly the music and drums, was very ritualistic and sensual. Now management was soft-selling us the ultimate in sensuality: to flaunt our naked bodies.

I never gave it another thought until the first preview show.

8

At rehearsals one day Lynn Kellogg announced that some money had been taken from her wallet. At first I thought it might have been someone who needed a few dollars and was too embarrassed to admit it. At that time most of us would have given anyone a loan. Then it got strange.

Gradually more money began disappearing in larger amounts. Someone among us was a sneak thief. We nicknamed this new and unwelcome member of the cast "the Phantom."

A lot of oddball, petty shit was happening. The Phantom became a scapegoat for all of it. First it was money. Then small but necessary props, like noisemakers, wigs, flags, and newspapers, mysteriously disappeared. Disappearing props led to missing costumes, then slashed costumes. The deeds of the Phantom got very heavy. There was someone sick in our midst.

That Lynn Kellogg was the first victim could have been spite. A lot of the kids referred to her as "the Corn Flake Heiress" because of her last name and her superior attitude. She was often late for rehearsals, and when she did take part she never seemed to work up a sweat like the rest of us or knock herself out. It was like the rich kid looking down on the poorer kids playing in the mud.

There was a rumor that management wanted to fire her during rehearsals because they didn't think she fit in. I seemed to be one of the few people who liked her. She was only doing her thing. And when Mal Williams, her manager, catered a birthday luncheon for her while we were still at Ukrainian Hall, everyone enjoyed it so much we were late for rehearsals. But that was nothing new.

9

Ronnie Dyson burst into the rehearsal studio, shouting, "Somebody shot Martin Luther King." We all stopped dead in our tracks. At first we assumed that Dr. King had merely been wounded, but a few minutes later we learned that he was dead and that the suspect was a white man.

Although the cast had its differences politically, we all got along well together and racial relationships between us were good. Suddenly, an invisible wall went up dividing the cast right down the color line: black vs. white.

I felt an anguish I can't describe. I couldn't stop crying for more than a few minutes at a time. Most of the blacks reacted the same way. The white kids stood silently, watching. I think a lot of them were confused. Although none of us knew Dr. King personally, he was one of the few black leaders everyone, black and white, respected.

Gradually my grief turned to anger, then rage. I felt torn apart. I felt that the White Man had killed Martin Luther King. If it weren't for the racist climate in this country, a man like Martin Luther King, a pacifist who preached nonviolence, would not have had to stand up on the bandwagon only to be shot down like a sitting duck.

I couldn't communicate with whites on any level for the next few days for fear of what I might say or do. The majority of the cast thought I was the most militant and hostile black person in the show, because from the start I let everyone know I wouldn't take shit from anyone, black or white. Now I was ready to prove their point.

I usually call the cards the way I see them. I've always been that way and always will be. A lot of the cast, particularly the whites, were not used to people being totally honest with them, particularly blacks.

Sally Eaton later told me that it hurt her feelings to hear I thought Martin Luther King had been killed by the White Man. She felt like I was accusing her personally.

Jonathan Kramer put it another way: "That day you didn't want to know about white people. Nobody did. It was very sad, but it passed, thank God."

I realize now that many of the white cast felt as badly as we blacks did. But at the time it didn't matter.

I wanted to believe we were a tribe. Not only because

of management's conditioning but because we all believed in *Hair,* each other, and the changing times. We knew it was up to all of us, no matter how small our part, to make it work. I wanted to see Peace, Love, Freedom, and Equality work. But a person also needs reality. He shouldn't be considered militant, rebellious, or hostile, the way I was to some extent, because he won't go along with the crowd. If you're right, eventually the crowd will see things your way. If you're wrong, same thing. It happened many times in *Hair.*

After Dr. King's funeral, things got back to normal. I quietly wondered why management didn't do anything openly to show their respect over Dr. King's death. After all, Dr. King was preaching the same things that management supposedly was. In his own particular way, he embodied much of the same spirit that *Hair* hoped to symbolize. It was the first sign of a crack in the dream.

10

The night of our first complete runthrough we changed rehearsal halls again, this time to The Hotel Diplomat. Everything there was super-rushed. Emmeretta Marks, Melba Moore, and I knew we were to be fitted for the "White Boys" number that night, but we had no idea what the costumes would be. Since the number was supposed to be a take-off on the Supremes, with three black girls singing about their craving for white boys, we all figured on gowns, gloves, and wigs.

Nancy Potts came in with some sequined material draped over her arm. She told us that it was our dress for the Supreme's number. Would we try it on? *Our dress?* When we first saw what it was, we were baffled. It was one large piece of stretch material with three straps attached to it. Nothing that anybody in that show came up with surprised me anymore.

Nancy said we were all to wear the one dress. All three of us shimmying into one dress was more of a sight than the costume itself. It was a little tight, but otherwise no problem. Nancy also gave us bouffant wigs ranging from light to dirty blond in color and three pairs of sequined, pointy-toe spiked-heel shoes. We looked like hookers.

Julie showed us some dance movements, basically a lot of do-wah-ditty hand, hip, and foot motions, which weren't too difficult to do, on solid ground. I thought the idea was brilliant.

Putting three women into one stretch dress that appeared at first glance to be three separate dresses, until the women suddenly sprang apart was an old idea of Nancy's. She was dreaming up outfits for us to wear when it came rushing back to her. Although it seemed perfect, she never expected Tom to go for it, but he did. "You know, I'm going to get blamed for this," he said. "I'm always putting three people into one something. . . ."

When we got to the Biltmore it was another song and dance, however. We had to put on the dress in a space approximately six by three feet. Our "dressing room" was the first landing of a kind of fire escape, screened off by a curtain. Once we had helped each other into the dress, we shimmied onto a plank made of wire mesh—and slowly the plank began to roll out over the foot of the stage. It must have been about ten feet high or so, but it seemed like the top of the Alps. We screamed. We were so scared we wouldn't do anything. It was like standing on top of a suspended subway grating on stilts. "If one of us falls it's all over" raced through my head. The plank-cranker rolled us back and we got off as fast as possible.

The real problem, aside from our terror, was the combination of wire mesh flooring and high heels. Some kind of plastic covering was placed over the wire mesh, but that only made it worse. Now it was slippery. Finally the shoes were eliminated. Still, we all carried on so badly—it was like singing from the ledge of a skyscraper—that they considered eliminating the dress altogether. But as we got more used to the idea, Melba and I realized we could probably make it work without the shoes if we had more rehearsal time. We told Nancy we were willing to try, but Emmeretta continued to fuss, carrying on like a banshee; she refused to do it at all.

Tom was so distraught he told Nancy to scratch the dress. He didn't want us upset for our first preview the next day. Neither did Nancy, but her face fell to the floor. The next thing we knew Michael Butler and Bertrand Castelli, the executive producer, were standing in the aisle asking what the matter was. Nancy explained.

Michael and Bertrand whispered among themselves for a while, then whispered to Tom, who returned to Nancy and said, "Let's try the dress one more time."

Keeping the dress was a big stroke for the show. It needed something to contrast the Army-fatigue and faded-denim look. Finally Emmeretta relented and agreed to do it.

Getting it on on that plank was a series of trial and error: our trial, their error. There was absolutely nothing to hold onto up there but each other, and Emmeretta was not that reliable. After more noise on the subject, a bar was installed so that we could hold on from the back.

One night one of the propmen couldn't control the plank-crank and it rolled out so fast we were all petrified. The minute it came to a stop, the three of us lurched forward, instinctively grabbing onto the bar behind. Otherwise we would have landed in the laps of the audience. I learned to grab that bar as long as the plank was in motion. Clutching the mike, the bar, and trying to maintain the surprise that it was one size sixty dress until we sprang apart mid-song became a real balancing act. To make matters worse, by the time we got to it, the plank was often strewn with flowers and confetti, making it even more slippery. Our complaints failed to get it cleaned off.

I guess I really failed in that exercise; I never really trusted anyone up there on that plank.

11

Everybody was excited by the idea of working with a full band for the first time. The day before our first preview we met them at Carroll Music Studios. I didn't know what to expect, nor did they, but I noticed the place was soundproofed; there was nothing to hold us back.

The band members looked like a pretty mixed group as they filed in, but there were a lot of suit-and-tie types. Galt, Jimmy Lewis on bass, and Steve Gillette on guitar had played the Off-Broadway show. Jimmy and Steve brought in most of the other musicians. Two, Eddy Williams and Don Leight, on trumpet, were recommended by the theater contractor. Another, Zane Paul, on clarinet and saxophone, was a friend of Galt's. The rest were Warren Chaisson, percussion; Alan Fontaine, guitar; Idris Muhammad (formerly Leo Morris), drums; and later, Neil Tate, alternate conductor and electric piano. Charlie Brown, on guitar, eventually replaced Steve Gillette, who later joined the cast as a performer before he left the show completely.

They were all great guys, but the one who stood out immediately was Eddy Williams. He was a big, jolly black man, over six feet tall, and appeared to be well over two hundred pounds. You knew when he was around by the way he talked and laughed: a lot and loudly. Everybody loved Big Eddy, and the whole band for that matter. They were the brightest spot in the show.

I dug Jimmy Lewis's playing the first night I listened to the Off-Broadway cast album. Idris Muhammad, who used to work with Sam Cooke, was one of the best drummers I'd ever heard. Later Idris' wife, Sakinah (formerly Deloris Morris), joined the cast.

After a while the band started to dress more loosely, but that day most of them had raised eyebrows over our appearance. Big Eddy later told me that he had no idea what *Hair* was about at first. He had done shows like *Yankee Doodle Dandy* and *The Boy Next Door*. The jump into *Hair* was mindblowing, "until," Big Eddy said, "the show got itself together." Then he thought it was the greatest thing he'd ever seen. Gradually most of the band began to dig the show. But during our first encounter they acted as if the lyrics were strange, we were stranger still, and the whole crazy scene was too far out. But when we got into the singing, they looked at each other in amazement; there was nothing strange about the sounds coming out of us.

When Lamont Washington—he played Hud, a kind of pioneer black hippie militant—sang "Colored Spade," I thought Big Eddy was going to pass out, he was laughing so hard. He could hardly play and it broke us up. Eddy was still laughing over Lamont's rendition of the song after the show opened. You could always hear him over anybody else in the band. Unlike most Broadway-show bands, ours did not sit in an orchestra pit but played onstage, seated in a hollowed-out truck.

Galt worked with the band much the same way as he had with us. He let them play the music in their own way, and while the chords and rhythm remained the same, their unique interpretations gave it something extra. Galt said he never liked to play the same thing twice: "I even change some of the accompaniment."

Of all the different elements in the show, the music meant most to the cast. We felt that if the music fell apart, the show fell apart. No one anticipated any trouble with the band.

One of the guys in the cast expressed my feelings when he said: "The music is what really pulled me further than anything else. I wanted to sing that music."

While we were going through our number at Carroll Music Studios, the backstage crew at the Biltmore was going through theirs—prop organization and lighting cues. We all met them later that evening for our first technical rehearsal-call at the theater.

From the beginning, backstage with the stagehands of *Hair* was like a battle between the Hardhats and the Hippies. One in particular had a real attitude. He thought the show would never be a hit. To him it was against everything he believed holy—Applepie-Americanism. We were warned to stay away from him, but he and his pals didn't do much to hide their contempt for us. I must admit I didn't do much to hide mine for them either. After four months or so we all warmed up to one another; we just got used to each other.

The stagehands were union men. They were there to do a job and that was it: "This business is money and nothing else. It's based on a buck!" To the cast, crammed so full of love and spreading the *Hair* philosophy, this was sacrilege. At the time there was still a vast difference between doing the show for Love and doing the show for Love of Money. But the minute the money started rolling in, the former went out the window and the latter took over. Everybody went through changes—except the stagehands.

To them we were just a bunch of "freak amateurs," totally undisciplined onstage and off, who looked at the show as a Way of Life, not just a job. They seemed to resent the fuss over us. "The Movement is not new, the name hippie is," they grumbled. "We did the same things when we were kids, only we were considered bums." To them, the whole thing was a well-organized freak show and the stagehands deserve medals for coping with the changes, idiosyncrasies, and problems. That *Hair* was not "frozen"—the same show performed nightly, without variation—bothered the stage crew most of all. It just wasn't done.

One of them said they were prepared to meet ordinary actors, professionals, but instead they found a "bunch of children." And that's the way we were treated for the most part. Some of the kids goofed on the stagehands-as-father-image, but I thought the lack of communication between us and them was one big hassle.

The stagehands of *Hair* were partly what the show was about. They were where they were at, and that was where they were going to stay. With one or two exceptions, they were jealous of the kids. They saw themselves reflected in the Father-Mother scene in the show, and, as one guy in the cast said, "It blew their asses."

Sal Briglia, the master electrician, and Harold Larkin, the spotlight man, were different. They were like the Will Rogers of the stage crew. They loved working with us and thought *Hair* was the greatest show ever to hit Broadway. Sal said it had rounded out his way of thinking; he understood his own kids better.

The situation with the stagehands reminded me of something Tom O'Horgan had once said: "If we could solve this in *Hair*, we could offer it as a grand plan for any civilization to work."

12

On the day of our first preview the cast decided unanimously to work the whole day, right up to opening curtain if necessary. None of us felt too sure about what we were doing onstage.

There was a team spirit despite the fact that some of us obviously pulled more weight than others. There were the workhorses and there were the sluffers; there were those on superstar trips and those just doing a gig. After a while who was what became all too clear. But, for the time being, we were all in the same boat. Most of us just wanted to be a part of the show.

Toward the end of rehearsals at Ukrainian Hall, Michael Butler appeared. With him was a man he introduced as a doctor who had offered to give us Vitamin B-12 shots. The management had agreed to pay for them.

I was immediately suspicious. Even if I hadn't been a nurse, sheer instinct would have told me something was fishy. The Good Doctor explained to us that the Vitamin B-12 shots were not mandatory. He emphasized that they "would not hurt" us and would give us "lots of energy."

To give us energy, I felt, a responsible doctor would have recommended a balanced diet and rest, along with vitamin *capsules*. He wouldn't suddenly appear with a hypodermic of supervitamins. Nor did the Good Doctor, to my knowledge, take any blood samples, listen to any heartbeats, or record any blood pressures.

In front of everyone I asked him what was in those shots. Averting his eyes, he mumbled something about vitamin compounds. As I've said, people who don't look directly at me when they speak make me uneasy. Then, in front of the cast, I asked him if there was anything else besides Vitamin B-12 in the injection. He said no and gave us a short but meaningless lecture on vitamins.

The size of the Good Doctor's syringe was something else. According to Jonathan Kramer, it was much larger than one normally used for vitamin shots. I tried to tell a few of the others what I thought, and some agreed with me, but I guess it was too soon for most of them to understand.

I'm too busy dealing with reality to get involved with drugs. Then again, I'm scared. A close nephew of mine died from too much dope. He didn't o.d., but overall the stuff destroyed him.

I had no intentions of taking the shots, so while the Good Doctor was doling them out at Ukrainian Hall I went up to Michael Butler and asked if I could have the money my shot would have cost instead. "Um, well, no," he stuttered. I laughed.

At least half the cast took the shots the first time, many for the same reason that I *didn't* take them: the suspicion, or knowledge, that there might be something more to the injection than Vitamin B-12. The Good Doctor and his magic syringe weren't dubbed "Dr. Feelgood" for nothing.

At first the Good Doctor came to the rehearsal hall a few times a week to administer the shots. Accompanying him were two mod-dressed assistants. One of them was unknown to me, but the other used to go to one of my acting classes.

Right from the beginning, some of the cast had always had their "ups" and "downs" (amphetamines and barbiturates), not to mention pot, to keep them going. The kids who took the Good Doctor's shots were definitely acting "up"; but after the first week or so, many of the tribe members became convinced that the injections contained a good deal more than vitamins—some who were taking drugs said they reacted to the shots much in the same way as they did to "speed."

Certainly the kids who took the shots had much more

strength and energy than they had without them. One of the guys who took one of the shots told me he had taken Vitamin B-12 from his family doctor. "Those [the Good Doctor's] shots were not just B-12 shots. B-12 boosts and enforces. This just sends you away."

One girl, who was overweight, used to rehearse with heavy plastic bags around her waist. "After the Good Doctor arrived on the scene she didn't need those plastic bags anymore," said Jonathan Kramer. Speed is an appetite depressant.

"I was willing to listen to the doctor," Jonathan admitted. "I don't think he knew what harm he was doing." Speed is addicting and people who get hooked on it can experience delusions, feelings of paranoia, and often severe depression. "The difference between what people looked like during rehearsals and eight months later was like going from *The Twelfth Night* to *Murders In The Rue Morgue*," John said.

A girl who used to work in both the doctor's and the *Hair* offices respectively, told me that the Good Doctor really believed in the shots at first. She herself used to take them. He thought they were some kind of chemical cure-all.

"Dr. Feelgood" gave his shots at 8:00 in the evening. The curtain, and most of the cast, rose at 8:30.

Considering the fact that one strobe-light sequence, the war scene, needed 108 lighting cues, that the cast of twenty-three people was onstage seven-eighths of the time, that the production used four hand mikes, five shotgun mikes, one wireless mike, and eight loudspeakers —the way the show came off was miraculous. There were no cases of hyper-stagefright, no serious accidents, and only minimum cue foul-ups. The show went very fast, and shots or no shots, we were all high from the reception it was getting from the first preview Broadway audience. They loved it.

13

Nobody realized it until it was happening. At the end of Act I of the first preview, Steve Gamet, Steve Curry, and Gerry Ragni all stood up nude. Everyone was momentarily shocked. Nancy Potts said Michael Butler was "as shocked as any of us. We'd really forgotten all about it with all the uproar, and they never did it at rehearsals."

The guys acted totally indifferent to the whole thing, as though they had been stripping for over a thousand people all their lives. I could understand why—each one had a beautiful body. Management happened to hire a cast which, with very few exceptions, was nice to look at with or without clothes.

For the first few previews the two Steves and Gerry were the nude stars of the show. Then two girls, Emmeretta Marks (nicknamed "The Body") and Shelly Plimpton, joined them.

Emmeretta said she did the nude scene because she wanted to see if she was "free enough," and at that point in the show it was very "relevant." More than that, she felt "a need to shed all my adult hangups." To her it was a supreme revolt.

Some of the kids didn't like being gawked at by the

stagehands at first. One night no one stood up and management ballyhooed with more talk of "liberation" and "relevance." Actually, the idea of the nude scene was catching on among the cast, but apparently too slowly for management. At one very heated rehearsal Michael Butler said that if more of us didn't strip, they would have to hire ringers—professional strippers—to do it. That made us all feel like the show would be a lie. It also planted a small seed in our heads: we were doing it for free, but they would have to pay ringers extra, wouldn't they? In the meantime, more of us stripped.

The Good Doctor's shots and the prospect of reviewers, agents, and talent scouts in the audience were also turning a lot of the kids on. But I knew of one guy, Erroll Booker, who was definitely being turned off, by the injections, at least.

Erroll, who was Emmeretta's male nude counterpart, said, "At first I was apprehensive about doing the nude scene. The shots 'shrivelled up my member,' as they say in Victorian novels. Not only mine, but you'd see all the dudes under the scrim pulling at their own, trying to straighten them out."

Most of the black guys were self-conscious about stripping regardless of the shots. It was partially due to the old cliché about how black men are really hung. They were embarrassed about getting too much attention on stage.

One black boy, who was nicknamed "Stud," got teased so much the first time he stripped that he never did it again. On top of that, one of the white girls practically raped him under the scrim while he was undressing while some of the male cast members looked on jealously. That was the first and last time he did the nude scene while I was in the show. In the long run, Erroll said the fact that he could stand up in public, naked, did him "an unbelievable amount of good."

Slowly but surely the number of nudes increased. I had no intention of ever stripping, but the more performances that went by, the more I wondered if I could do it. Then it became a real challenge.

On my first try I got as far as taking off my bra, only exposing my breasts. I thought I'd get cross-eyed from trying to stare down at myself. Were my nipples erect? Did my breasts look all right? Were they bigger or smaller than the other girls' standing nude on stage? How the boys felt about being compared to one another became evident. But from the moment I had decided to strip I had no reservations. Within three or four more performances I knew I'd undress completely.

My next step was taking off all my clothes, but holding the scrim waisthigh while I was standing. There were about seven kids stripping regularly the night I decided to go the whole route. Wiggling under the scrim, anticipating the cue to stand up mother-naked, all I could think about was holding my stomach in and, above all, what would the band say about my body? (I didn't care about the stagehands.)

The musical cue came. I stood up. What was all the commotion about? It was like taking one big skinny-dip into the ocean, only this was a sea of eyes. I never felt so free.

While you are up there you think every light and eye in the place is focusing on your naked body. The first time I saw the nude scene from the audience, I realized that, unless you knew us well, you could hardly tell us apart. Between the dimness and the flashing, whirling lights, you could barely distinguish the difference between male and female.

Some critics thought the blinking lights were a cop out. Even though I thought the nude scene relevant and beautifully done, if that stage had been one speck brighter I wouldn't have stripped.

Gradually most of the kids did it as a goof or an

ego-trip. A lot of them dug the exhibitionism. In fact the cast was more into nudity than the audience was.

The audience's reaction to the scene was one of embarrassment at first, and then just plain embarrassing. Some whipped out cameras, which was supposed to be "strictly forbidden" in the theater, every *Playbill* stated a warning. Most had binoculars. The real weirdos covered their eyes or bowed their heads.

Many waited especially for the nude scene, then said "It's disgusting!" and walked out in a huff. One time, two little old ladies sitting third-row center got up in the midst of the scene and walked out, holding onto each other, tripping up the aisle, backwards. They didn't miss a single second.

When there were nuns and priests in the audience, the nuns would usually scurry up the aisle, veils flying, while the priests remained glued to their seats. I heard that one woman in the audience whipped out rosary beads, blessed herself repeatedly, and mumbled "Hail Marys" the entire time.

The people with children were the most uptight. Some would try to make their kids close their eyes or stare at the floor. One mother hen tried to tuck the heads of her two children under each armpit.

The nude scene also seemed to attract the fringe element of nuts in the audience. During one performance, a young girl came from backstage naked and stood in the front of the stage, mingling with the rest of the nude cast. Most of us tried to act like it was part of the show. Afterwards, the same girl went backstage, headed straight for a male dressing room, and proceeded to go down on everyone who wanted it. She had a lot of takers, including one of the stagehands.

Another time, a nicely built blond boy, who was what we called a *Hair* groupie—the group of teenaged kids who used to hang around the theater—walked onstage from the audience without any clothes. Although he wasn't part of the show or the act, he turned, faced the audience, bowed, then joined the fully clothed cast. We tried to hide him from view. Someone covered him with a blanket then quickly led him offstage. When Fred Rheinglas questioned him, the groupie suddenly dropped the blanket and ran naked out into the street. We never saw him again.

I don't think people should flaunt nudity for the hell of it, but when it's relevant, why not? *Hair* was the first Broadway show to present full-bodied naked men and women face to face onstage. It paved the way for shows like *Oh! Calcutta!* and *Dionysus '69,* which made *Hair* seem like playing in the sandbox as far as nudity was concerned.

Given an inch of skin, the public wanted a mile. It was packing them into the house.

During previews, RCA records, which recorded the Broadway cast album, threw a press conference for us.

"The story is hard to follow. What are you trying to say, anyway?" one reporter asked.

"We're not asking you to follow anything," one girl in the cast said. "Just try to dig what's going on."

"Do you really think people will take to male nudes on Broadway?" another reporter asked.

Tom, Gerry, and Jim fended the questions as best they could. The rest of us in the cast got a little crazy and hostile, not so much by the squareness of the questions as by the righteous attitudes behind them. For a second I thought we were being interviewed by the stagehands. Here we had worked our asses off to give them a great performance and all they were worried about was the story line and the public viewing of male genitals. At one point a reporter asked us who were the real as opposed to the fake or professional hippies.

Despite the fact that some of the kids were picked out off the streets, like Sally and Shelly, I don't believe any of the original Broadway cast members were real hippies. The potential was there, and many tried hard to make it, but none did.

Gerry and Jim ran around making promises and spreading the *Hair* truth; Steve Curry, Steve Gamet, and Shelly acted like the perennial Summer of '67 "Love" children. Some, who were cautious and suspicious at first, like Leata Galloway, wound up "searching for what Tom was telling us"; another, Suzannah Norstrand, thought the whole exercise-ordeal was like "torture, a self-endurance test"; and one, Erroll Booker, who joined the show in July, thought that "forcing people to deal with their insecurities, putting people through that many changes, was destructive."

No matter how you wanted to look at it, we were twenty-three talented nobodies living under a flimsy veil of Love who had been brainwashed into thinking we were the harbingers of a new dawning, the Aquarian Age.

"We were all suffering from the same disease," Jonathan Kramer said, "ambition and eight shows a week. *Hair* was probably the most exhausting show ever put on Broadway."

Whether we wanted to or not, we had to believe, or act like we believed; otherwise there was just no way we could go out and do that show every night.

14

The preview audiences for the most part were hip. A lot of kids who didn't catch *Hair* Off-Broadway wanted to see it before it became big-time boffo. Mainly, they seemed to enjoy themselves and were very uninhibited about letting us know it.

We had more trouble with some—though not all—of the ushers than we did with the audience. The opening act of *Hair,* as mentioned, called for the cast to mill around the audience, mingling with the people. Then, on the cue, or vamp, from the band, we proceeded to the stage in slow motion. The whole thing took approximately five minutes. Although most of the audience was already seated by this time, both the cast and the ushers were told *we* were not to move for latecomers, but to let *them* move around us.

It was a successful piece of staging and the audience really seemed taken by it. There's a little bit of "ham" in everyone, and during that scene some theatergoers let it all hang out. Some would grab a cast member and dance with her or him in slow motion; others would try to mime the slow-motion action on the way to their seats. One night, one woman got so carried away she joined us onstage for part of the opening number.

All the ushers were aware of the rules of the game, but it didn't stop some of them from deliberately cramping our style. Many of them would bump into us or push and yell at us to "get out of the way"; others would purposefully block our way, or even put us down in front of the whole theater by calling us "creeps," "weirdos," or "dirty hippies."

One night, when an usher told me bluntly to get out of her way, I told her she had "an attitude." Heatedly, she said that after *Hair* I'd never get another job, that I was a dirty no-talent hippy. That did it. My blood was boiling. I'll take anything I deserve, but this was uncalled for. I read her right then and there.

Her eyes filled with tears, and she ran up the aisle and out the theater. The audience probably thought it was part of the act. She left the job a few weeks later. As the show grew older, we had less trouble with the ushers.

Although none of us were aware of it at first, there were a number of bomb scares when the show first opened. We thought all the cops hanging around backstage were there simply to keep things under control and to check out the nude scene. But during one particular performance, when the stagehands came wandering onstage, a few even climbing the scaffolds, it was obvious that something was up. None of the cast paid too much attention, but I suspected that something serious was wrong. When I left the stage to get some props I asked the stage manager what was happening. "Oh, it's just a bomb scare," he said, "but we don't think anything will happen."

Despite his blasé attitude I fought strong urges to run out of the theater. Instead I hung very close to the edge of the stage, as did a few others in the cast. Giving the bomb scare the benefit of the doubt, I still thought most of it was a big bluff. Where were the men in hooded asbestos suits? And why would management endanger the lives of an entire audience, never mind the cast, if they really thought a live bomb was ticking somewhere? Watching the stagehands creeping around so casually looking for a bomb, I thought the whole thing was dumb. Nevertheless, it made us feel uneasy.

On a couple of nights the show didn't start until after the time the alleged bombs were scheduled to blow up. People were warned not to enter the theater. Only one cast member refused to do a show because of a bomb scare. He admitted he was scared, and split. Fortunately the bomb scare hoaxes passed.

Who knows, it might have been the work of the Phantom.

15

Thirteen days till opening night. The countdown was logged by one of the stage managers.

April 12: Tension and energy levels down a bit. Thus, show not as consistent.

April 16: Extra performance waiver signed today.

April 19: Diction problem still. Not enough time spent on diction. Talk to Osorio [Richard Osorio, the company manager] about cancelling shots after opening. False up-and-down effect on performance. Stage managers very uptight about not playing the same show twice in a row, and *cast.*

April 20: Sound problem still not solved. Sound man good—too many mikes onstage. Rehearsal wasted this A.M.—tough on company with little result.

April 21: 11:30 rehearsal. Theater not opened till 11:50. Work on war sequence. Serious problem arising from not doing same show twice in a row. Day off badly needed by company. Particularly as no day off *next week.* Quite a bit of experimental goings-on—props added. "Climax" cut, "Bed" added.* Director uptight—instant changes are cutting momentum of show.

April 22: Planned day off.

April 23: Planned cancellation of performance. Rehearsal in place of it. Morning rehearsal twenty-five minutes late. Continued technical with added props . . . instant cuts and improvisation. "Dead End" cut. So much for Sheila.**

---

*In one scene, Sheila was supposed to strip and make love to Claude onstage on a real bed. Claude sang "Exanaplanetooch," Sheila sang "Climax." Neither worked, so both were cut and "The Bed" was added and sung by the chorus. This scene was always being taken out, then put back in or rearranged. But it just never worked, and Sheila remained a virgin throughout the play.

**Originally Suzannah Norstrand sang "Easy To Be Hard." "Dead End" was cut because Lynn Kellogg had trouble singing it, and she was given "Easy To Be Hard" instead. Suzannah cried and cried; to pacify her she was given the understudy part of Jeanie, a pregnant girl who sang "Air," a song about air pollution. Sally Eaton, who played the part on Broadway, had originally played it Off-Broadway. When Sally became pregnant, the part was adapted to her condition. After Sally had the baby, Jeanie remained "pregnant" onstage. I had previously asked Galt and Julie if I could audition for the part of Jeanie's understudy. Both said yes, but before I got a chance the incident with Suzannah took place. I was mad, but that's show biz, I figured.

April 24: Rehearsal 1 to 6. Director added motorcycle today.* (No motor.) Propwise we have enough room left offstage to add one more elephant and that's it! Wigs to be fireproofed this weekend.

April 25: Rehearsal reverts back to 12 and 8 hour rehearsal period. Can work four hours only. Extra rehearsal waiver signed today. Cut "I'm Hung"—no one bothered to inform anyone else. No motorcycle tape sound yet—jurisdiction problem on speaker placement. We are losing control . . .

April 26: Show supposedly "frozen" tonight. With four hours of rehearsal left on Sunday and three hours on Monday, it is not a bad idea.

April 27: Mat. 2:30. Co. call 7:30. Rehearsal cancelled—wonderful, wonderful.

April 28: Voice coach to be here from 7:30 to 9:30.

(It was the night before the big opening. Steve Curry, Shelly Plimpton, and two others in the cast spent the night in the Biltmore Theater. According to an interview with Shelly in the New York *Times* (9/13/70), they hid in the balcony until the night watchman left. Tom knew they were staying all night. "It was for good luck. It was like spreading good vibes throughout the theater." The next day they said it was spooky.)

April 29: Entire cast got penalty pay, two-eighths salary, for working on the day of opening night. Rehearsals disintegrated into being a security activity for the director. Not a hell of a lot accomplished. Full crews were called.

---

*In the scene following the "Electric Blues" number, Claude, dressed in his gorilla costume, entered the theater riding a motorcycle. The motorcycle was eventually cut, because the propmen had to be paid $50 extra every time they moved it.

Five extra men were hired just to shop for electrical fixtures. Money was no object.

We rehearsed from three to five. At five, the Good Doctor came in with his black bag of tricks. "He made us feel like he was Santa Claus," Paul Jabara said.

16

"... the talented Tom O'Horgan has staged the production with a feeling for speed."
—RICHARD WATTS, JR., New York *Post,* 4/30/68

Incense and psychedelic lighting flood the lobby as well as the theater and stage. There is no curtain to hide the lights, pipes, and scaffolding, or Robin Wagner's pop-art set.

The audience files in. The cast is scattered all over the theater. I watch how the cast deals with the opening-night audience: each is trying hard to out-do or be more clever than the next one. Mingling with the audience is supposed to be ad-lib—the sky's the limit—many are half-naked; some wriggle around on the floor in the aisles; some ask "are there any drug users or homosexuals in the audience?" This gets a few snide replies. Most hand out flowers and incense, throw confetti and corn, or just talk to the audience, which looks puzzled.

When we hear the vamp for the slow-motion number, everyone freezes. Then we inch our way to the stage. The vamp comes right in the middle of an action, a word or a sentence, and we suddenly stop right where we're at, which startles some of the audience. They don't know what's happening.

The band moves into its truck on stage. Jim Rado sits cross-legged on stage. Shelly walks on slowly, holding a grill. At the same time, another girl enters from the opposite direction carrying a blanket. The grill is placed on the blanket in front of Jim.

The electronic sounds of chimes and bells can be heard. Then Gerry, wearing a loincloth and Indian head-dress, somersaults onto the stage. He cuts a lock of Jim's hair, and Lynn Kellogg burns it in the grill. The band moves on to a driving Rock beat, picking up momentum. Ronnie Dyson lets loose with "Aquarius."

I break out in a rash of goose bumps on the first note. His voice spreads out over the audience, which suddenly stiffens in their seats. They remain that way, stiff, throughout the entire show.

The opening night audience is not at all like the preview audiences. Looking out at them, I think they resemble a display case of middle- to old-aged hippies. An assortment of psychedelia abounds—see-through shirts and blouses, suede, leather, fringe, beads. They look like they are at a costume party, or as if they desperately want to be part of the act. None of them would dare wear those clothes to any other Broadway opening show. The downtown look is invading uptown, but tonight it seems pretentious.

Whether the audience is turned on or off by the show is impossible to tell. They appear controlled. The preview audiences let all hell loose when they dug something. This one sits like they're stone cold.

"I thought, 'What is wrong with Michael Butler bringing in all these *old* people, these charity-ball benefit types, on opening night?' " Jonathan Kramer said. "They didn't crack a smile, didn't laugh. Nobody responded at all."

Neither Jonathan nor I are on the shots, but three-quarters of the cast is and people are speeding by like a drag race in a city traffic zone. Things are happening too fast. The kids seem to be coming from every direction all at once—climbing up catwalks, swinging out over the audience on ropes, hanging from the balcony. I speed up my own actions just to try to keep pace.

"I don't think anybody saw anybody else opening night," one guy said. "It was such a conglomeration of egos—everybody pushing to get out in front. Everybody wanted to be noticed."

Many of the cast don't feel they are ready for opening night. Some aren't sure of their lines. But the show is so fast that much of what actually happens is lost in the speed of the performance.

All I can think of is not to let anybody upstage me. I don't think we are giving our best performance. Most of the show is blanked out the minute it happens. Before each one of my lines I make a mental sign of the cross and say a quick prayer that I won't forget them; I don't.

Near the end of Act I, seven nudes, including myself, stand up. After the nude scene, all the lights in the theater are shut off. There is a whirring sound of sirens which seem to be getting closer and closer to the theater.

As the sirens scream louder, the theater lights are cut back on. The audience assumes it is intermission.

Suddenly two cops appear, one onstage, another in the balcony. "You're all under arrest!"

Just then the lighting men up in the booth happen to look out and see the cops. Although they never heard the sirens, they put one and one together—we all know we could be busted at any time—immediately cut their own lights, and drop to their hands and knees. Frantically they try to figure out a way to get out of the theater until one of them happens to notice that the balcony cop is barefoot. He's a member of the cast. They are so relieved they just laugh it off.

One of the band members, on the other hand, quietly collects his music and instruments the minute he hears the approaching sirens. Seeing an unguarded side exit, he is almost out the door when he is stopped. Someone tells him the sirens are just from passing fire engines. Still suspicious, he reluctantly hangs around. "I really thought it was a bust," he said later. "Man, I just wanted to split."

One of the electricians said, "I was dumbfounded, but I finally recognized one of the 'cops.'" The scene is a total surprise to them. The audience titters, and it's really intermission.

The second act flies. At the end of the show, we sing the hand-holding finale, "Let The Sun Shine In." The stage lights go off. It's anybody's guess as to what the audience thinks.

I can't believe it. They are giving us a standing ovation. We are a hit! The applause rolls over us like a tidal wave, and I lose count of the number of times we are called back (with no curtain, there are no traditional curtain calls). They are still yelling "Bravo" while we are changing in our dressing rooms.

Michael Butler, all grins, gives the entire company bead necklaces. To Fred Rheinglas, he gives a necklace made out of Indian-head nickels, which he wears. Some of us wear Michael's gift; some of us don't.

I later read that under the impression that *Hair* is

a flop, Michael Butler's father sent his representatives around to withdraw his interest from the show on opening night. Michael Butler is on his own. So far so good, but what the critics say becomes crucial.

Afterwards there is a party at Ondine's, a discotheque on East 59th Street. I go with a friend of mine, Jackie Britt. The one person in the world that I want most to be there, Ted Landry, the guy who set me up for my audition with *Hair* in the first place, is nowhere to be found.

I expect Ondine's to be like a Sardi's, theatrical, but it is a dark, cocktail lounge-type place with a small dance floor in back. With the exception of cast and management, I can't see the faces of most of the people there. Someone tells me that supposedly Richard Pryor, the comedian, and Rudolf Nureyev are roaming around, but I didn't see them.

I would have preferred a smaller, more intimate opening-night party. The atmosphere of this one is loaded with a "here-we-are-mixing-with-the-freaks" hilarity. This kind of crowd and attitude is not my thing.

Robert I. Rubinsky is so bored he pulls out a joint and smokes it. Everybody is shocked. Pot-smoking in public is daring in the spring of 1968. But soon, people follow his lead, and as the party wears on, almost everyone begins to smoke in the open.

There are a lot of backers at the party, and most of the bad vibes I feel can be put down to sheer worry. Their only concern is the critics. The cast is so high for the most part that they don't care about anything, even the reviews. None of us are anxiety-ridden. We all strongly feel it will either be a big hit or a big flop; no in between.

Around eleven o'clock everyone gathers around a small television set to watch the reviews on newscasts. They are all raves. We all cheer after each one.

Someone brings in a New York *Times,* and Bertrand Castelli, who has a heavy Corsican accent, begins to read Clive Barnes' review. He is so excited his accent becomes progressively thicker. We can hardly understand him.

"Let someone who speaks English read it," Elsie Dyson yells. Michael Butler takes over: another rave.

Assured that *Hair* is a hit, half the people leave the party, and then, narrowed down to the cast and their friends, it really begins as far as I'm concerned. Everybody is soaring. Diane Keaton is so drunk she can hardly stand. Jackie Britt takes her home in a cab.

The entire cast is overjoyed with the reviews, but the full impact doesn't hit me all at once.

It takes me a while before I realize we are all going to have to deal with each other as members of the cast in a hit Broadway musical as well as members of a "love tribe" for a long time to come.

17

Hair, as everybody knows, had no real plot or rigid story line. It was made up of a series of episodes, loosely strung vignettes, which focused on one topic or another—the Vietnam War, drugs, sex, parents, the Establishment.

For me, the lack of formal plot helped create the feeling of the play, and that's the way Tom directed it. *Hair* was a total experience, something that involved you as you watched it.

Since *Hair* was virtually a different show every performance, it's hard to pin down one final and "frozen" version of what each audience saw. The performance we gave opening night comes closest to the "authentic" one.

The first thing the audience noticed was the set. There were no stage curtains—everything onstage hung right out. *Hair* was performed on what's called a raked stage, a stage set at an angle. It was painted gray, and printed in white on it were such phrases as DEAD END and NO SMOKING. The set, designed by Robin Wagner, was placed mostly upstage to give us a lot of room to move around. Stage right stood a tower with a fire escape-like contraption; a stairway led to different levels, each of which had various props—an old bicycle horn and other cycling paraphernalia; a papier mâché Santa Claus; a juke box, etc.

Hair never really had a starting point, or traditional "opening." At 8:30, the time printed on the tickets, the cast was dispersed throughout the theater—in balconies, on ramps, climbing the catwalks, in the orchestra, walking on the backs of seats, and even onstage. The idea was to create an immediate rapport with the audience; after all, the atmosphere of *Hair* was supposed to be Universal Love. The things we sometimes had to go through to do the show were incredible.

ACT I

All during the warm-up, or vamp, one character, Claude, remains onstage. Dressed in pants, polo shirt, and fur vest, he sits cross-legged, Indian style. If *Hair* had a protagonist or hero, Claude was it. Next in importance was Berger, Claude's best friend. The rest of the characters, or tribe, unraveled with the action of the play.

As the audience trickles into the theater, the burning grill is ceremoniously set down in front of Claude, and at a musical cue, the cast freezes and then proceeds in slow motion to the stage.

Berger, assisted by Sheila, a student protester type, cuts a piece of Claude's hair and burns it as a sacrifice. The cast forms a large circle and Ronnie Dyson breaks into "Aquarius," heralding a new age, the dawning of Aquarius. I'll never forget when just after Ronnie had let loose with the first few lines, we heard a voice from the back of the theater shout: "Sing, baby, sing." It was Elsie Dyson, Ronnie's mother, the all-time Stage Mother of the Year. But that was nothing compared to the time we had two Claudes sitting onstage at the beginning of the show: Jim Rado and Steve Gamet. The show was ready to start and they both were arguing about who would do the part. It took a good deal of coaxing from the stage manager and some members of the cast before Steve Gamet finally gave in.

Berger strips down to his briefs, wanders about the audience, and returns to sing "Donna," a fast rock number about a sixteen-year-old virgin whom he misses. While singing he swings out over the audience on a rope, like a hippie Tarzan.

We then divide into groups to sing about different drugs—hashish, cocaine, heroin, opium, LSD, DMT, STP, and so on. Then, seemingly without transition, we form into different religious poses--the Madonna and Child, Christ on the Cross—while Woof, another pal of Claude's, sings, as if it were a church hymn, "Sodomy," a song about different sex acts—fellatio, cunnilingus, masturbation, everything in sex that's considered "dirty."

Hud, a pioneer black hippie type, is carried onstage by two white boys hanging upside down from a pole (whenever I played Hud, I could never seem to get off that pole without falling; anyway, it always got a laugh). Hud sings "Colored Spade," listing the stereotypes people have labeled blacks—colored spade, nigra, black nigger, jungle bunny—while three black girls "tar" (mud) and feather Claude.

While he is being washed clean of mud and feathers, Claude sings "Manchester." Then Hud, Woof, and a new tribal member, Dionne, sing a song about have-nots, "Ain't Got No" (homes, shoes, money).

Sheila enters as if on horseback and Hud hands her a poster. After her song, "I Believe In Love," the protest rally begins with Sheila, as leader, asking the cast what they want. Cast: Peace! It became chant.

A trap door in the stage opens and out pops Jeanie, who sings "Air," a song about air pollution. Once, while playing Jeanie, I forgot some of the lines. I just sang something like: "ell ome ocohol." I mean I just went blank. That had to be my most embarrassing moment with the show. At the end of the song, Jeanie climbs out of the "manhole" to reveal she's pregnant by a crazy speed freak, and is in love with Claude.

The cast, as though in a classroom, sings "Initials," a fanciful tune about LBJ taking a ride on the IRT downtown to the Village, and then Claude engages in a dialogue with three sets of mothers and fathers. The moms are men and the dads women and their exchange is a satire on parents in general. Finally, Claude sings, "I Got Life," a wistful celebration of the life within us all.

Berger makes a dramatic entrance by jumping from

the tower. (After a while he tried it bellywopping into the arms of the cast. In the beginning there were eight or twelve people to catch him, but people started dropping out for one reason or another and sometimes he'd dive with only four cast members below. I thought he was crazy to take the chance. The jump was some nine feet high.) Berger tells us he's been expelled from school, sings "Going Down" while three school principals with Hitler-type mustaches do a spoof on schools and education.

Claude enters, and we learn he's passed his Army physical and is about to be drafted. A tourist couple come up from the audience, and when the woman asks: "Why the long hair?" Claude and Berger lead us into "Hair," the play's theme song, if there is one, which enumerates every conceivable type of hair and hairtype. The tourist lady, apparently beginning to see the light, sings "My Conviction." When Berger makes some comment about her dress, she says she's not wearing one and flings open her fur coat to reveal she's clad only in a pair of jockey shorts. "She" is a "he" in drag.

The first time Jonathan Kramer, as the tourist lady, pulled this stunt, it caught us as much by surprise as it did the audience. We collapsed with laughter, and continued to do so because he played it so differently every time. Jonathan was a very funny guy.

After singing "Sheila, Franklin," Sheila, who digs Berger, gives him a yellow satin shirt. But he gets angry, rips up the shirt, and Sheila sings "Easy To Be Hard," about how cruel people can be to one another. (I'd agree with most cast members that Diane Keaton was the best all-around Sheila. But the first few times Melba Moore sang the song even the cast applauded. What a voice she had!)

As Claude tries to cheer up Sheila, Jeanie re-emerges

from her "manhole" and gives the audience a run-down on who's hung up on whom: Jeanie on Claude, Claude on Berger and Sheila, Sheila on Berger, Berger on everyone, and Woof on Berger, though he says he's hung up on Mick Jagger. This is followed by a spoof on American flag worship—"Don't Put It Down"—in which Woof, Berger, and another tribal member pay mock tribute to the flag (which is actually bunting), folding it according to Army regulations. The cast descends into the audience supposedly on their way to a Be-In but to wind up backstage for costume changes.

I remember at one performance there was a well-dressed, distinguished-looking old man sitting in the orchestra in an aisle seat. As the cast walked up and down the aisle distributing flowers and pamphlets he would try to hit or trip us with his cane. He hit the girl in front of me and was about to deal me a blow when I gave him an evil look and said, "If you hit me with that cane, I'll make you eat it." When someone threatens me, I forget about Peace and Love. He kept up his antics throughout the show but never lost his mind enough to hit me.

Crissy shows up, and in one of the rare, quiet moments in the show, sings of her love for "Frank Mills." The tinkling of bells offstage is the cue for the Be-In to begin. The cast enters from the wings in colorful costumes—less hippie street-gear and more together, as though everyone has dressed up for the occasion. As we sing and dance to "Hare Krishna," a table with a small grill is set up and some of the boys burn their draft cards.

When it's Claude's turn, he refuses to burn his. Suddenly, everything stops. The entire stage is covered with a scrim, and while Claude sings "Where Do I Go?," those of the cast who have decided to strip, do so under the scrim. At the cue, the nudes stand up singing "Beads, Flowers, Freedom, Happiness" in dimmed lights. It was also the cue for the audience to whip out their cameras and binoculars. We felt that cheapened the whole thing and many times the culprit would be caught when the nudes pointed to the spot from which the flash bulbs went off. Once I saw two elderly ladies sitting in the front row sharing a pair of binoculars.

Sirens are heard in the distance, getting progressively louder. All the theater lights are cut, the cast exits and the house lights flash back on to an empty stage. Suddenly what appear to be two policemen announce that everyone in the theater is under arrest. The audience is informed that it's

Intermission
ACT II

Hud walks onto a dark stage carrying a wind-up Victrola. Crissy listens to an old Kate Smith recording of "White Cliffs of Dover." A spotlight picks up four cast members dressed in mirrored costumes. They begin to sing a hard Rock number about the media, "Electric Blues," as the rest of the cast enters, flashing flashlights. Then the whole stage, cast, and music goes wild under a multitude of strobe lights.

Once again the stage is darkened for "Oh Great God of Power," a spoof on Con Edison. (This was one of the most dangerous scenes in the show. The cast carried candles on the dark stage, and people could be seen tripping over steps and each other in the darkness. One night the hair of one of the black girls, who always wore an extra large Afro, caught fire. It was a near tragedy that turned comic, because the moment "her" hair started to burn she ripped it off—she was wearing a wig—and stomped out the fire. But it wasn't funny when Shelly Plimpton's long hair caught fire and she didn't know it. Luckily I saw it and smothered the fire.)

Claude roars up from the audience on a motorcycle, dressed in a gorilla costume, growling at the audience and cast. He takes off the gorilla head to reveal who he is and tells us he's just returned from the induction center. Everyone tries to make a joke out of it. Berger and another guy create a mock scene of what happened to Claude at the draft board. Claude gives Woof a poster of Mick Jagger, as Woof tells us how hung up he is on the entertainer. Three white girls sing "Black Boys," about their preference for black men, which is followed by three black girls in a red-sequined dress and blond fright wigs who sing about "White Boys." The whole "White Boys" number is a spoof on the Supremes. In the middle of the song the three of us suddenly step apart to reveal we are all wearing one large stretch dress. During previews "White Boys" came first, but the number was such a show stopper that "Black Boys" was anticlimactic, so they turned it around.

Berger hands out "joints" to the cast and everyone turns on (sometimes using the real thing). The stage lights are dimmed and the cast sings "Walking In Space," about tripping on drugs. This was one of my favorite parts of the show because I dug the music and enjoyed the dancing.

Claude's trip begins. Under dimmed lights, five guys do an Army number; the lights come up and Berger, now George Washington in powdered wig and robe and followed by six or seven members of his "army," all girls, is ordered to retreat. He rides offstage, and four Indians—Tonto, Sitting Bull, Crazy Horse, and Little Beaver—shoot down the "army" with bows and arrows. But General Grant, in Rebel uniform, appears, resurrects the army which now consists of Abraham Lincoln, John W. Booth, Calvin Coolidge, Clark Gable, Scarlett O'Hara, Teddy Roosevelt, and General Custer. Lincoln is the only one in costume. He's (I'm) wearing a fine brocaded velvet jacket, red, white and blue stockings, and a raggedy top-hat. "His" hair is also braided with white ribbons. They (we) dance a minuet and are attacked by three African witch doctors. The head witch doctor, Hud, has a confrontation with Lincoln (me), then the three witch doctors break into a song about freedom and emancipation, after which Lincoln recites a mock Gettysburg Address while a white girl shines "his" shoes (sometimes with her hair), The trio sings "Happy Birthday, Abie Baby," then pretends to shoot Lincoln. But instead of falling, Abie says, "I'm not dying for no white man."

Four Buddhist monks enter wearing long robes. One is supposedly set on fire, and three Catholic nuns strangle the remaining monks with their rosary beads. In quick succession: three astronauts kill the nuns with ray guns; three Chinese kill the astronauts with knives; three American Indians kill the Chinese with bows or toma-hawks; three Green Berets kill the American Indians and each other with machine guns. The entire scene is then repeated in reverse and original sequence under strobe lights. The lights come up again and a sergeant is reading a roll call. Two parents are talking to a suit on a hanger as if it were their boy in service.

A childlike tune is heard in the background. The cast starts playing children's games, which slowly evolve into simulated war games that get pretty frantic. Once during this scene I got pushed off the stage. The cast sings "Three-Five-Zero-Zero," a surrealistic anti-war song. The words are whispered, then build in pitch, finally yelled in a freak-out. Meanwhile, two members of the tribe are watching from the tower. They sing "What A Piece Of Work Is Man," a verse from Shakespeare set to music. Still singing, they descend from the tower and walk around the bodies onstage. The song ends and they too fall down. Then everyone in the cast sits up as if awakening from a dream, sings a few lines from "Walking In Space," and Claude's trip is over.

Sheila, trying to escape the reality of Claude's pending Army induction, sings "Good Morning Starshine." When Melba Moore sang the song the band cooked; I thought I heard instruments I hadn't heard played before in the show. Four boys carry in a mattress on top of which is Crissy while "The Bed," a song about the various uses of a bed, is sung by the cast.

The cast says good-bye to Claude. An Army sergeant is waiting as Claude backs off stage, singing "Ain't Got No."

The cast re-enters from all sides playing instruments—garbage cans, sticks, garbage-can tops, flutes, etc.—which build in rhythm and intensity as we go into a "Hell no, we won't go!" bag.

The cast freezes; Claude appears dressed in Army clothes with cropped hair. He sings the opening of the finale, "The Flesh Failures (Let The Sunshine In)," but none of us can see or hear him. He talks to Berger but Berger can't hear him. He then sings a reprise of "Manchester England" and is joined by a trio which sings "Eyes Look Your Last." Finally the whole cast comes to life and covers Claude's face with their hands, and he lies down slowly as if dying. We surround him. (Sometimes this was a pleasure because we had so many bad Claudes!)

Sheila sings the first verse of "Flesh Failures" and we all line up at the foot of the stage to sing "Let The

Sunshine In." Everybody's doing their own thing—holding hands, waving their hands, etc. We eventually walk offstage, singing. Claude is revealed lying onstage as if dead.

That's basically what the audience saw . . . that first night at *Hair*.

18

We were called "dirty," "outrageous," "orgiastic," "fun," "bold," "ballsy," "wild," "dynamic," "youthful," "naive," "simplistic," "fresh," "an experience"—and a "smash."

Hair was reviewed from Schenectady to Long Island on opening night—and in London the day *before* we opened on Broadway. Since then, the show has been written about, criticized, and analyzed in hundreds of publications around the world.

Almost all the opening night critics remarked on the nude scene at the end of Act I but were quick to point out that it wasn't as shocking as their readers and listeners might expect. But just mentioning the word "nude" was enough to make people sit up. Some of the critics warned the show wasn't for everyone, especially kids —they seemed to forget that, for the most part, that's what we were—and that many people might be turned off by the flag scene, the nude scene, and "that four-letter word." The day before the opening, the Sunday New York

Times said we were "more explicitly physical and profane" uptown than Off-Broadway. Although true, this was not the point of the show.

Nearly every review sang praises for Tom O'Horgan. Galt's music and Gerry and Jim's story and lyrics were also mentioned, but it was definitely Tom's thing. In fact, a few weeks later the Sunday *Times* devoted a front-page story in the theater section to him. Some critics picked up on a few of the cast members for special mention; in her *Show Business* review, Joyce Tretick said I had "a voice to remember." Other reviewers commented favorably and unfavorably on my "Abe Lincoln" number. But we were usually taken as a tribe, treated as one. On November 2, 1968, the *New Amsterdam News* had a long writeup about the surprising fact that more than one-third of us—ten—were black, a rarity on Broadway.

The Big review, and one of the earliest, was Clive Barnes' in the New York *Times* on April 30, 1968. In his usual restrained manner he said: "I think it is simply that it is so likable ... the essential likability of the show is to be found in its attitudes and its cast." He called us "the first Broadway musical in some time to have the authentic voice of today rather than the day before yesterday." How much more "in" could we get? In an article published later in the *Saturday Evening Post,* he said our success was "inevitable" even though we broke every rule in the book. Broadway would eventually have to catch up to Off-Broadway—and street theater—and we were just helping the transition along.

Walter Kerr was not as enthusiastic in the Sunday *Times* on May 19. He liked it, but felt we had "lost something in innocence" since the Off-Broadway days: "What's happened is that the occasion has subtly grown older," he said. And hipper.

In general, opening night reviewers felt the Broadway show was freer, better, and livelier than the Off-Broadway show, but *Newsweek* also felt we'd lost something in our trip uptown and added an unwelcome "taint of camp and aggressive put-on."

Not all the reviews were up. The *Daily News* review of the opening, written by John Chapman, was one of the few bad ones we got. He liked the songs, dances, and "zestful abandon of the young cast," but said we had "stunk up the theater with incense and dead flowers" and made a "racket." After admitting that " 'Tribal love-rock' is not my type of music" and suggesting as a title "The Dirty-Foot Follies" because of our bare feet, he concluded, "*Hair* is no show to take a lady to." On the other hand, *Variety* recommended us for teenagers.

Richard Watts was also not too turned on by us in his New York *Post* review. *Hair* was not "strong enough in its moments of propaganda . . . and some of it seems uncomfortably amateurish and a little tiresome." He had us pinned. How could we "amateurs" relay "propaganda" we ourselves were beginning to doubt?

New Yorker thought we were all hype but "a joyous hell it is. Well worth visiting, and even, if you have the strength, worth living in." *Saturday Review* advised theatergoers to stick around even if offended, to "be rewarded with a remarkable experience" in "multi-sensual theater" that "so vigorously challenges Broadway convention."

We were even reviewed by the *Wall Street Journal*. John J. O'Connor was subdued but predicted "the form will be important to the history of the American musical." That was pretty right-on.

A lot of reviewers picked up on the idea that *Hair* would revolutionize theater. On opening night on WMCA radio, Peggy Stockton said we were "the first of its kind, a Rock Opera." Mike Stein advised WNEW radio listeners to "forget everything you've ever thought of as a Broadway musical comedy," because *Hair* "sweeps Broadway like a breath of fresh hair."

We were something else, and they loved us. We were *Now:* "the one current show which exactly reflects the temper of the times," said WOR-TV's John Wingate.

Stewart Klein called us "a gas" on WNEW-TV. "There are dirty words in *Hair,* and naked people, and disturbing ideas," he said. "But there is also a freshness, a zest, and a charged effervescence that no musical has had on Broadway this season." Even when we were "sloppy, vulgar," we were "terrific," said Len Harris of CBS-TV. Our plot may have seemed to him "sentimental and old fashioned," but he still voted us the best musical of the Broadway season.

Soul Illustrated called us "free theater." In the Sunday *Times* of May 12, William Kloman hailed the show as a "celebration" which might help the generations communicate, the same way *West Side Story* did years before.

After Dark devoted their June cover story to *Hair,* which they said was a "very, very healthy" show. "It's so much fun, I almost wish I was in it," Neal Weaver said, coming close to the attitude of the *Hair* groupies.

Life said we "represent the protest of youth to remain unshorn of its ideals," a refreshing musical which might "lure people back to the musical theater they long ago deserted."

Two years later, on March 1, 1970, *Gay* magazine said our "mass communication" might not have changed anyone's life-styles, but we certainly turned them on and planted "the seeds of that change."

And on the second anniversary of our production,

in its April 17, 1970, issue, *Life*'s "Parting Shots" reviewed the success of *Hair* companies around the world and said: "In some ways, being in *Hair* serves as group therapy."

We were really a mixed bag—all things to all people.

But some reviewers caught on to what was really going down: In his September, 1968, *Harper's* magazine review Robert Kotlowitz, who also called us a rock opera, labeled the show "a sellout . . . only in a commercial sense, for there are purists of the psychedelic world in lower Manhattan who believe that the show has really sold out to the enemy camp uptown, which continues to buy tickets in unending quantities."

The San Francisco *Chronicle* said that although a breakthrough, "the old established practice of eyeing the box-office seems just as much to have influenced the creators as the stirring up of revolution."

And when some word of our "revolutions" backstage reached reviewer Colette Dowling of *Playbill,* she wrote in September, 1968, "Is it all professionalism and sham, this production that seemed to spit so brightly in the eye of the Establishment?"

Ironically, in Michael Smith's *Village Voice* review on May 2, he said *Hair* had been "betraying everything it was trying to represent" when the show was at the Public Theater, but that Tom O'Horgan had fixed it up for Broadway. While over in London, Alan Brien's *Times* review said the best thing about the show was "the way it can mock its own pretensions, satirize its own philosophy." Maybe this was an omen.

Leonard Probst (of NBC News) thought "the twenty-three young men and women work with such conviction that you're sure they're for real . . . and not actors who will call it a night after the curtain comes down."

Little did they know. . . .

19

After the show was officially labeled a hit—"the West Side Story of the sixties"—people began to copy our lifestyle onstage, offstage. More and more imitated our way of dressing, listened to what we had to say, and acted like we, and they, were always on. We became Instant Celebrities. Everyone I met who had heard, or was told, that I was in *Hair* was automatically fascinated by what I had to say, what I did. My own style—of dressing and doing what I felt like doing rather than what was expected of me—changed. I became much more aware of myself, less self-conscious.

Nearly everyone in the cast was ego-tripping to some extent, but the rest of us would bring them back to reality if it got out of hand. Not so with Gerry and Jim.

In the beginning Gerry and Jim were like part of the cast. Although they both claimed to be twenty-six years old, they seemed older than the rest of us. As the "authors," they didn't take any special privileges; they worked just as hard as we did. We all felt we had a rapport with them. Gerry, especially, horsed around a lot with us. Jim was always more aloof. During rehearsals he was unapproachable and sent out vibes that said "Don't touch." He wore a blond long-haired wig, and many felt that was part of the reason.

But the more of a thing the play became, the more of an ego-trip they went on. It wasn't what they'd do so much as how they were doing it. They couldn't seem to handle what was happening. As one person put it, "they were up to the pubic hair in success."

There was a great deal of ad-libbing and improvisation while we were getting the show together. Not everyone was good at improv, but those who were good were encouraged to do it. It was part of our training. Much of the ad-lib and improv during rehearsals was eventually written into the script.

"The rehearsals were where we wrote the show," Jonathan Kramer said. "The rehearsals were rewrites."

It was rare to see Gerry or Jim without a tape recorder or Gerry, especially, without a pencil and pad. I often used to take along a journalist friend of mine, Didier Delanoy, to the Haymarket, a theatrical hangout. He noted that everytime he saw Gerry there, he was writing in a note pad.

Gerry and Jim were on many of the cast members' shit lists because, all things being "equal" in *Hair,* we felt we should have gotten some sort of written credit (even a group footnote on the credit page in the Playbill) for our separately small, but large when combined, contributions to the script. We weren't after money but mere public recognition or "thank you" for our efforts.

Most of the parts in the show had been given out by the time I joined the cast. Although I enjoyed being in the chorus and acting as one of the Supremes, I wanted to do more. I had no idea that I'd be asked to do "Abe Lincoln" until it happened.

One day during rehearsals Tom was picking various people to do small roles. "You do this," he said to one; "You do that," to another; and to me, "You do Abe." The idea of a black girl playing Abraham Lincoln did not really surprise me. The interchanging of male and female roles in the show was already established, and the part of Abe had been played by a black girl in the Off-Broadway *Hair*.

Getting the part of Abe made me feel I was finally going to be doing something as an actress.

At least I had to *look* like Abe, and I had a line.

During Claude's trip on acid in Act II, General Grant calls the roll, and when Lincoln's name comes up, I say, "Present, Sir." That, in two words, was it.

One day, during one of our five-minute rehearsal breaks, Lamont Washington, Donnie Burks, Ronnie Dyson, and I started fooling around, doing some fifties Rock vocal riffs. When they got the background together, I began to recite what I remembered of the Gettysburg Address, but instead of doing it straight, I interjected lines like, "All riii-ight . . . ," "Sock it to 'em, baby," "Tell it like it is," and so on. Some of the cast gathered; most thought it was funny. Gerry Ragni encouraged me to do more, and then asked Tom to come over and watch us.

I recited as much of the Gettysburg Address as I could remember, the first few lines, ad-libbing the "hip" talk in between every other sentence. Tom said to keep it in the show and to write out the Gettysburg Address including my ad-libs.

The group and I experimented with it and it worked. I wrote my lines into the Gettysburg Address; they were written into the script and put into the show. However, Tom always allowed me to change it during a performance. The scene only became a "set" part of the script when new assistant directors came in to replace Tom. Otherwise, we were encouraged to develop our parts, which kept much of the show spontaneous.

Lamont and I started experimenting with his role as Hud. He'd say his lines to me, and I'd throw cracks back at him. For example, he'd tell Abe how he's going to "cut" Abe up, because he hates all "You white mothers." And I'd say, "Now wait a minute Amos or Uncle Tom or Uncle Jemima or Snow Flake or Stepin Fetchit, I'm one of y'all." Lamont: "Well, what the hell you doin' here, mama?" Me: "Would you believe takin' a sun tan or pickin' cotton or tobacco or doin' light housework?"

Any or all of these were put into the show. Right up to Lamont's last performance, we played around with improvising. It was usually very funny and fresh. After he was gone, the lines—our original improv—sounded formal and stiff, because those who followed weren't as creative with the part as he was. One of Lamont's cast nicknames was "Peter Professional."

"I wrote the Young Recruit," Jonathan told me. "It was also my idea to open the fur coat and only be wearing a jock for the Margaret Mead number. I don't do improv anymore. *Anywhere.*"

Robert I. told me that he nearly freaked out after seeing the show nearly a year after he had left it. There was a take he used to do, a guitar-twanging Rock musician motion he used to do alone. When he returned to the show, not only was his replacement doing it but everyone else was too.

Almost everyone in the cast made a contribution to the show. It was that kind of play. Within the hang-loose framework, whatever you said, if it was funny, if it worked, was used.

Paul Jabara, who was with the Off-Broadway cast, said that in the beginning he wanted to get as much of his mind into the show as he could. He admitted that neither he nor I had much of a part to begin with—he played Mom—but by the time we opened, we both had good parts because we created them. He said that seeing everything he ever said in the show translated into the language of others, without an ounce of credit, was depressing.

Paul had approached Gerry and Jim about it once, and they denied that the cast wrote anything. They said that they wrote the script. Paul drafted a letter to Michael Butler to the tune of "give us some credit," but nothing ever came of it.

Many thought the so-called "message" of the "book" was just used for pep talks. Robert I. thought "the story was passé from the very beginning."

Jonathan Kramer once said, "The dialogue is dime-store pap. We're the show." And many of the reviewers also noted that the "story," "book," and "plot" of *Hair* had all but "virtually" disappeared.

Like everything else with *Hair,* it was often hard to say where Gerry and Jim's script left off and the cast's improvisation came in. No one in the cast was trying to take away from their thing, rather they were adding to it, and no credit, no recognition, no *nothing* for those who helped pull it together was a bring-down.

A few days after we opened, Fred Rheinglas, the production stage manager, talked to us about keeping the show tight. There was too much camp going on, cueing was getting screwed up. Fred even sat down and typed out our first *complete* script in two days. For a while the camping around was cut to a minimum, but eventually it came back, led by Ragni and Rado, of course. Gerry and Jim would change the dialogue and blocking onstage according to their whim of the moment. They would also call extra rehearsals to make their parts better, then show up late. Most of the cast was getting annoyed, not to mention that just being on that stage was simply getting dangerous.

Gerry was a wildman onstage. He would get so carried away he'd literally step on people. Many refused to work with him; I wouldn't take his roughhousing. One night while I was dancing on my knees for the Be-In, Gerry stepped on my foot—it wasn't the first time. I got mad and said, "If you step on me again I'm going to kick your ass." I was never stomped on again.

I don't think Gerry was aware of himself onstage. He would try to curb his roughhousing, but before long he was right back at it. It was almost as though he were possessed. As part of the War scene, Gerry used Natalie Mosco as a "bayonet." He got more and more carried away until he was in danger of battering her head on the floor. Natalie had to complain to the stage manager.

Lynn Kellogg was someone else who said that Gerry manhandled her. One day at the end of a matinee, she gave Gerry such a rabbit-punch in the ribs that he was moaning and groaning in pain. I touched the sore area and asked him if it hurt? "Yes." If he wasn't hurt it was a fabulous performance, but most of the cast thought he was faking it. After a visit to the doctor, Gerry returned to the show all bandaged up.

Slowly but surely Gerry and Jim stopped socializing backstage. Most of the cast thought they were becoming Establishment. Whenever there was a problem between cast and management, they would pretend to be on the side of the cast, but when push came to shove, they wound up on management's side. On the other hand, in any dispute between themselves and management, they expected us to rally behind them as a "tribe."

We had tribal meetings with the "chief" to work it all out. About once every two to three weeks, the stage manager would receive a smoke signal from the "chief to the tribe" via telex, and would notify us that one was coming up.

I thought the producer's willingness to meet with us to discuss our problems was a good thing. The only hitch was that he usually came surrounded by a blanket of people, mostly members of the "inner-tribe," his cronies. With the exception of Joe Cavallaro, Bertrand Castelli, and assorted production staff, many of the faces were familiar but remained nameless.

In the beginning the tribal meetings were very democratic. First we listened while the chief ran through his number, the *Hair* credo—"We are a Love Tribe" and "Rules are meant to be broken"—then we raised our hands and waited our turn to speak. But after a while they degenerated into free-for-all bitch sessions. Most of the time when we asked Michael Butler a question, one of his cronies would answer instead. The chief was never to blame for any of the problems of the tribe: it was always someone else—stage managers, the business office, *kismet*.

One of the most heated early tribal meeting gripes was the lack of a water fountain and a shower backstage.

Backstage was a mess. There were five dressing rooms for twenty-three people—later there were more. Gerry and Jim had one; and Steve Curry, who played Woof, had another. The rest of us were left to sort it out in the remaining three dressing rooms—three *small* dressing rooms. We were living like sardines. We also had two johns, more like water closets, to share between us. Second only to the stage, they saw the most action. After a while, unable to stand the filth, I used the stagehands' john downstairs.

At the start of the show someone began scribbling graffiti all over the walls with magic marker. The place looked like the inside of a subway car.

To top it off, you had to be constantly on the lookout for dog shit. Some of the cast brought their pets to the theater during rehearsals and shows. I like animals, but only when there's enough room for people. Sometimes the smell of dog shit was overpowering. Eventually management barred all pets from the theater.

Among other things, *Hair* was both a sweat- and a thirst-making show. Without a water fountain (near the stage) and a shower facility, the cast was dying of thirst onstage and post-performance filth off. I used to carry Life-Savers with me all the time, especially onstage, to ward off dehydration. During one scene in particular, we were smothered in steam rising from holes in the stage. Whatever they used to make the steam smelled like roach spray to me and was making some people sick. One girl claimed it made her hair fall out.

It took management nearly a year and a half to install the water fountain and two showers.

Another favorite topic at early tribal meetings was Steve Curry's dressing room. Since, with the exception of Gerry and Jim, we were all packed in like oranges in a crate, I wondered why Steve would rate one whole room to himself? Woof was only a minor lead. Most of the cast was curious. "Steve has a special clause in his contract stating that he can have his own dressing room," we were told. In the beginning nobody said much. After a while, the subject dominated our meetings. It was simply unfair.

Although Steve Gamet and Shelly Plimpton unofficially shared Steve's dressing room, reducing our crowd by two, we were still living in a crush. Steve had personalized his dressing room by fixing it up with psychedelic posters, red light bulbs, and other head paraphernalia. As our gripes got heavier, management finally told Steve that he couldn't have the whole room to himself. He had to move.

Steve Curry and Steve Gamet threw a temper tantrum that rocked the foundations of the Biltmore. They completely demolished the room, not even sparing some of their own personal stuff. I had heard that both Steves were fired after that incident, but were rehired when the damages were paid. We were glad. Steve Curry was an essential part of the show, none of us wanted to see him go. The next day the room was put back together again; Steve Curry moved in with Gerry and Jim, and Steve Gamet and Shelly both went to their original dressing rooms. The empty dressing room was divided between five or six people. It was still a squeeze, but more breatheable.

20

Sally Eaton gave birth to a boy in the Good Doctor's office. The majority of the cast, plus a photographer from *Avant Garde* magazine, were on hand to watch. I didn't go because I had seen so many births that the only other one I ever want to see is my own baby's. Sally was put out by my absence.

I asked her why she let *Avant Garde* cover the birth. "Because I thought it was a beautiful experience that could be shared with a lot of people. We should not be afraid of the miracles of birth, death, and sex."

According to *Avant Garde,* Sally took "no anesthetic and no inducement, just mental concentration on the sheer animal joy of the experience."

"I never took LSD while I was pregnant," Sally told me. "I took it to have the baby because it's made from ergot—and they've been using ergot to induce contractions since the Middle Ages."

Some of the cast used to call Sally Eaton "the Poor Man's Raquel Welch."

Sally came of age on the Lower East Side around the time Tuli Kupferberg was still a Fug, and something called the "Sexual Revolution" was getting underway. Tuli Kupferberg wrote a book called *1000 Ways to Make Love,* which, Sally said in an interview with *Screw,* greatly influenced her ideas toward fucking.

Gerry and Jim discovered Sally when she was still modeling on the Lower East Side at a place called the Village Theater (later called the Fillmore East). When they saw her she was half-unwrapped in a sari. She sang three songs semi-naked, accompanying herself on guitar. They dug her and sent a note backstage: "Work N.Y. Shakespeare Festival. We like you and want you to try out for our play."

Sally claimed to be the biggest hippie in the show. As far as free love was concerned, she went overboard to prove it. As far as I was concerned, there was only one real hippie in the cast, Barry McGuire. Barry (of "Eve of Destruction" fame) joined the show in May 1968 to understudy for the part of Claude. He seemed to genuinely love everybody and vice-versa. Nobody had a bad word for Barry. The *Hair* groupies used to flock around him backstage; he loved to advise them. Barry knew what he wanted and he didn't bullshit about it.

Together Barry McGuire and Sally Eaton were two of *Hair*'s less inhibited members of the Love Tribe. About 7:30 one night, when people were returning from their in between show breaks, Barry and Sally performed their famous fucking scene for all Broadway.

The whole thing started when Jonathan Kramer said to Barry and Sally, "I'm sick and tired of hearing you two speak of love, love, love. I want to *see* it."

Barry hesitated at first, then suggested that Jonathan ask Sally how she felt about it.

"Sure, I'm game. Why not?" Sally said.

People not only lined up to see the exhibition, but many ran out to get friends, even from other theaters, to come watch. Many of the band members from *Hair* were among them.

A member of the stage crew claimed that he went to shut the door and Sally yelled at him to leave it open.

". . . we hocked away at every conceivable position," Sally told a *Screw** interviewer, "grunting and groaning and laughing and straining and coming. He [Jonathan Kramer] watched my face when I came."

It was just about over when I wandered into the theater. There was a hubbub among the cast: "Did you see *that*?"

"See what?"

"I've never seen anything like it!"

"Like *what*?"

Sally later said that a lot of the cast were disgusted

*Sept. 22, 1969

and turned their heads away. She thought the stagecrew were "hipper" than the "hippies" in the show, because they, apparently, didn't turn away.

"I've been in show business for more than twenty years, working in everything from flop joints to the best nightclubs. I thought I'd seen everything," one of the band members said. Another one told me he went out and got drunk later that night: "I looked and I didn't believe it. That sort of thing belongs downtown, Off-Broadway."

Allegedly, when Barry and Sally had finished fucking, they looked at the crowd of on-lookers as though they were a bunch of fools.

Sally didn't feel that she and Barry were being particularly "exhibitionistic." "It's simply saying sex is a beautiful thing and people should be able to do it," she said. "Anywhere. In the middle of Times Square if they like." As for the cast members who left in disgust, Sally didn't think there was as much sexual liberation among the cast as legend had it. She wondered "where they're at to think that sex is disgusting? ... There are some people who have to feel sex is dirty before they can climax. That's how sick they are. I can come with anybody. . . ."

Almost everybody looked down on Sally, but not Barry, for the fucking show. The kids in the cast who tried to act the most cool about it, like it was nothing new, were the ones with the most questions, the ones who made the biggest fuss.

Whether you wanted to or not, most of the time you wound up being a Watch Queen backstage. When I say we were exposed to sex in *Hair* I mean it never stopped. Usually the same eight or nine people were always involved. They were the ones who were most into drugs and every other kind of outrageous trip. The gay ones were flamboyant, nicknaming each other "The Wo-Man" and camping around. The straight ones, or the ones who thought they were straight, weren't so sure after a while.

These kids carried on out of boredom, or because they were expected to do it, or because, as Paul Jabara said, "Everyone's sickness was brought out." For many of them, *Hair* created a special kind of environment that didn't exist anywhere else.

A lot of the guys, and some of the girls, always walked around nude backstage. There was a time when you couldn't go anywhere in the theater—hallways, dressing rooms, the balcony, and especially the johns—without falling upon two or three members of the cast doing drugs or having sex, or both. There were any number of gay or straight combinations.

One guy, Robert I. Rubinsky, who had never had sex with a woman before, was sucked off in the dressing room by one of the girls in the cast. Robert I. said that he was "very happy that it was 'the Queen' and 'not a faggot queen' who did it."

The so-called orgies at the theater were another part of the *Hair* myth. More like group-gropes, they usually happened in one of the dressing rooms. Several cast "orgiasts" would come into the theater early—or sometimes stay late after the show—smoke a lot of grass and then wind up balling each other all over the dressing room floors. Erroll Addison Booker and another guy in the cast were invited to the "orgies," but "there was nothing there" that either one of them wanted.

"They were into orgies like a twelve-year-old is into masturbation," the one guy said.

Robert I. confessed that he didn't go to one particular orgy—an early one—because he was "afraid of being rejected." He was afraid they'd tell him, "Get out! We don't want to fuck with you."

Neither did I, but for completely different reasons. However, one day I came close.

I was sitting in my dressing room drinking tea with Natalie Mosco. I needed some sugar so I went upstairs to borrow some. The door to the first dressing room I came to was closed. I never go through closed doors without knocking first. Nursing taught me that you could walk in on something you might regret.

Knocking on the door, I heard sounds of scuffling and muffled voices. Steve Curry poked his head around the door. All the lights were out inside.

"Come in," he said.

Although I wasn't exactly sure about what was happening, I wasn't about to find out by plunging into a dark room.

"I just wanted to borrow some sugar."

They were out of sugar.

Later, Jonathan Kramer, who was part of the scene, told me what had happened. There were five people, two girls and three guys, in the dressing room. One of the couples were into each other. Sally Eaton was just making the rounds. Everybody was waiting around for someone to do something.

"I was there," Jonathan said, "because one of the girls carried on about me lusting after her guy. He wasn't gay, but as long as Sally was there hanging on to his joint, he was willing to let me give it to him. So the three of us had a little ménage à trois.

"Julie Arenal walked in, said, 'I don't believe it,' and walked right out again.

"After it was all over I said to this girl, 'I have just *had* your boyfriend.' She didn't forgive me for two years."

During one picture call for the *Saturday Evening Post,* however, Jonathan Kramer refused to do drag. He played the part of Margaret Mead on stage, and he didn't want to become publicly known as a drag queen offstage.

Shortly after we opened, a few of the girls in the cast and I were sitting in Sally's dressing room when Paul Jabara walked in. He was whining and carrying on, almost crying: "I'm so horny. I can't get an erection."

While explaining how he had tried practically everything to get a hard-on, he unzipped his pants, pulled out his cock and started massaging himself.

We all sat there, dumbfounded, watching him jerk-off. His heart wasn't in it.

"Sally, can you help me get it up?"

Sally put down her make-up, went over to Paul, and went down on him. She was really working him over; meanwhile, he was still belly-aching about his problems, both life and sexual, in general. I didn't hear a word he said. We were all riveted to our chairs watching Sally giving head.

After about five minutes Paul said, "Forget it, Sally, it won't work." Paul put his limp cock back into his pants and left. Sally went back to her dressing table and resumed putting on her make-up. You would have thought she had just finished washing her hair.

Nobody said anything. What was there to say?

The nearest I got to group sex at the Biltmore was the tease sex we did in the show. This came during Act I right after Sheila sings "Easy To Be Hard," and Berger rejects her present of a yellow shirt by jumping on it and repeating the word "sex" over and over again. At that point the whole cast jumps on each other and is supposed to act out simulated sex acts: hugging, humping, touching, flirting. I always did it with the people I dug—Erroll Booker, Steve Curry, Ronnie Dyson.

At a given point we're supposed to stop the tease

sex, but one night my partner, Ronnie Dyson, just wouldn't stop. I started fighting with him: "Stop it, Ronnie. Stop it!" He was like a madman. I finally had to slap him on the face. Meanwhile, the entire theater, spotlight and all, had zeroed in on us. The audience thought it was a scream.

Sex was so rampant intramurally, whether in groups or individually, that those involved couldn't understand my indifference.

"There were people like yourself," Erroll Addison Booker said, "that nobody knew anything about. Everybody had rumors about you, but nobody knew. You were smart enough to keep your sex life out of the theater."

A couple of the girls in the cast asked me if I was gay. During one evening performance, Sally Eaton calmly told me that she wanted to eat me and make love to me. That she'd been thinking about it for some time. I told her I didn't want to hurt her feelings, but that I wasn't into women. "I hope you don't put me down for telling you," she said, "because I really dig you."

Sally wasn't a dyke, but she was obviously not what you'd call "straight" either. She said she was bisexual. In her own words, "I don't know if I'm perverted or advanced, I really don't."

It was hard to say. Sally's brand of sex was her own. There was one particular gay girl in the cast whom she wanted to go to bed with, but the "ethos of lesbians," she said, "seems to be that girls want to get involved in some kind of personal relationship." They don't cruise each other as freely as gay guys do. Sally said she didn't prefer women out and out; in fact, she thought, "as a theoretical idea, it was better not to have a preference for either sex, but to go equally with both."

When a girl in the cast came on to me, I can't say

I felt anything. I feel they have a right to do as they please, but I don't have to be involved.

Occasionally, some of the kids in the cast—gay and straight—and I used to go to gay bars, mostly for the dancing. Except for decor, all bars, gay or straight, strike me as being the same. But the gay bars were looser. You could really let yourself go on the dance floor, which is what I dug.

One time we were all sitting around a table, when a black girl wearing thick horn-rimmed glasses tapped me on my shoulder and said gruffly, "Let's dance." Depending upon the music, I have no objections to dancing with girls. If it's a fast tune, all right, if I want to. If it's an "up against the wall tune," as we used to call the slow numbers, I prefer a guy.

"No thank you," I said, then turned back to the group. Still hovering behind me, she would not take no for an answer.

"Why won't you dance with me?"

Since I happened to be the only girl in the group, the guys were all laughing their heads off. She wouldn't leave me alone.

Finally I said, "Listen, miss. I just don't want to dance with you. Does that make it any clearer?"

I don't think it did. She glowered at me for the rest of the evening.

One of the lesbians in the cast used to come on to me all the time. I'd just shrug or laugh it off, because otherwise I liked her. She was going with another girl in the cast, who was nicknamed "Good Neighbor Sam," and they had a little clique. Mostly they stuck to themselves.

When a guy in the cast came on, that was something else. The gay guys never made passes, although they teased a lot. The "bisexual" and "straight" guys in the cast, and production staff, came on all over the place. I usually turned them down, although I didn't always want to. I found out the hard way that having affairs, no matter how short, with guys you directly work with, is dumb. Someone always gets the short end of the stick. One time, though, passion did get the better part of reason.

John Aman, one of the later members of the cast, gave a party. We had the use of an entire three-story brownstone. The specialty of the house was a nine-foot foam-rubber bed which was lit up by lights underneath. The heat from the lights made the bed warm and comfortable. Everyone tried it.

Throughout the evening different people tried to get some group action going on the bed. At one point, Gerry and Jim kept asking me to take off my blouse. I told them to "Get in the wind." There were a couple of guys sitting on the bed hugging each other, but that was the extent of the "orgy," for the time being.

Nothing happened until near the end of the party when the center of the activities changed to different rooms. Since I love to be warm, I remained on the bed talking and teasing one of the boys from the show who was nicknamed Stud. Although he was attractive, he never really turned me on sexually.

He was fooling around, trying to convince me that I should sleep with him then and there; I was fooling around trying to convince him otherwise. I happened to notice that the other two couples, male and female, in the room were fooling around with more conviction than we were. Both couples were half-undressed.

I knew what was happening, but I was so inside the scene that I felt myself becoming more and more outside of it. Almost unconsciously, what little clothes they had on were slowly being discarded. The eroticism of the room—the soft lights, the warmth, this guy's fabulous body—was arousing. When he started pulling off my clothes, and as I lay there saying no for the hundredth time, I finally just gave in. Why not? The other couples were really getting into each other.

John Aman came in at one point, then left, quietly closing the door.

When it was over we all just got dressed.

Apparently similar scenes had been going on all over the house. "Stud" wanted to come home with me, but I didn't want him to. I had no regrets, but it was just a thing of the moment.

21

What *Hair* did to shake up traditional Broadway theater is unprecedented. Michael Smith, a *Village Voice* critic, said it had ". . . blown up Broadway." Tom O'Horgan admitted to me that he wouldn't go that far, but he did say that he could "afford to be even more outrageous uptown" than downtown.

Our controversial director was a very busy guy. In addition to the Broadway *Hair,* Tom was directing the Los Angeles, London, San Francisco, and Chicago productions of *Hair.* He had also directed two "experimental" Off-Broadway plays—Paul Foster's *Tom Paine* and Rochelle Owens' *Futz*—nearly piggy-back to *Hair.*

While often strange to many of the cast, the pre-rehearsal sensory exercises were something Tom had been honing and developing for some time. He seemed to know what he was doing, even if we didn't, and for that reason the cast always went along with him. He exerted a soft-spoken, even-tempered—except for an occasional "Dammit!"—control over us, which made us come together as a whole. We weren't aware of the discipline behind Tom's methods while it was happening.

When Tom O'Horgan left the show, shortly after we opened, what little discipline we had left with him. I lost track of all the assistant directors, production stage managers and stage managers who came and went. For the most part, with the exception of Michael Maurer and Marc Weiss, they were like bad copies of Tom. They would have been better off not trying to imitate him. Not one was as good as he at overseeing group dynamics, and when they tried to explain what they were trying to do, it never made any sense. Tom could always tell you why he was doing something.

Even a bad reaction to one of Tom's exercise numbers was better than the *director* trips his replacements tried to lay on the cast.

None of the new production staff seemed to know what the "story" was about. All the love, freedom and spontaneity it expressed onstage came from whatever Tom had established and the cast could create. All the magic went out of the show when new people came in because they tried to change it. They tried to *direct* scenes and force their interpretations on our heads. And when the cast tried to explain something in return, they became even more uptight. We would tell the acting assistant director that as soon as Tom returned, he was just going to change his changes back again, so why waste time, but it never did any good. They wanted the "love children" to suddenly turn professional, while at the same time maintaining the *Hair* myth.

To those of us who were in it from the beginning, the whole process was tiresome. We would work with the assistant director for a few rehearsals until Tom reappeared from one of his other activities. Then he would take us through scenes from the show, or exercises, adapting and often adding something new, but never wasting time. Every time he came back to work with us, periodically at first, then less frequently as time went on, the performances were a hundred percent better. From the start there was always a certain honesty about him, and he never seemed to change. After months he could come in and pick up right where he had left off.

When Heather MacRae, daughter of Sheila and Gordon MacRae, first came to the show, replacing Diane Keaton as Sheila, she said, "I don't think you can know everything there is to know about *Hair,* unless you were there in the beginning. I know why you [the original cast] were picked. I could see it. You all grew, loved, and hated together."

"After three or four months," Tom said, "the honeymoon is over. You realize it's a darn hard show I'm doing eight times a week. You come up against the problems of living, doing the show, and trying to keep yourselves together for it. Any professional actor would only give a certain amount of himself to a performance, knowing how to space himself over that period. This is something we intentionally didn't want to have, and in doing so we were asking for trouble. No one can give the kind of stuff the kids in *Hair* do and hold up. You just can't.

The fact that the show gets into trouble is a human process. The honeymoon is over because the cast becomes more sophisticated. . . ." Or the staff becomes less so.

New staff also didn't know how to put new cast members into the show. Usually these new cast members felt uptight, as though they weren't a part of "the tribe" and wouldn't be accepted.

One guy said that when he and a girl first joined *Hair* right after we opened, most of the kids resented them. It was like a "carefully developed paranoia." They didn't know who the newcomers were; they didn't know what parts they themselves were going to play. They felt themselves and their positions in the show threatened. As it turned out, the two new cast members were swingers, people who play more than one part.

Without leadership, rehearsals deteriorated into terrible fiascos, then grinds, then depressing, futile drags. The workhorses bore the brunt, because the same seven or eight of us were the ones who wound up listening to a repetitious lecture.

After a momentary bitch about the absentees (who needed the money most), the acting stage manager would tell us the agenda. If it involved choreography, it meant trouble immediately. We spent most of the rehearsal relearning routines which we knew would be changed right back to what they were originally as soon as Julie showed up. Whenever we tried to tell the dance assistants that they were teaching us something utterly new, they'd resent it, insisting that "this is the way Julie told me to do it!"

Even working with Galt became a chore. It was not his fault, but, of course, nine out of ten times the people who really needed to rehearse were not there. The understudies would practice the part the right way, and then the absentee would show up for the performance and sing the part the wrong way.

Not long after we opened, Galt left the show. "I didn't stay to conduct the show because it takes so much time . . . I wanted to write some more stuff." Apparently, there was no replacement to assign understudies for singing parts; that left it up to whoever was acting stage manager. He usually had little knowledge about who could sing what, and often a cast member got assigned a part just by asking for it. More often than not, the choice was bad.

Even if two understudies were assigned to a part, the absentee rate was so high that before the week was over, a third often would have to be temporarily assigned.

Every once in a while, management would reprimand the cast with warnings and threats. Things would get back to near normal, or at least normal for *Hair,* until everything would begin to degenerate again.

Management had been so busy breaking Establishment theater rules that they finally had to create some new ones. First they started docking the pay of latecomers and absentees without solid excuses. Then they began giving attendance bonuses of $10 per week to cast members with perfect rehearsal and performance attendance records. Attendance improved somewhat, but not for long.

According to another Equity rule, cast members could be excused from rehearsals for another paying job, something that didn't interfere with the performance—like talk shows, commercials or modeling—so long as it was reported to the stage manager before rehearsal time was posted. Proof wasn't necessary. The cast began lying about extra jobs, so management began posting rehearsal schedules as much as three weeks in advance, instead of the customary practice, the night before. The new *Hair* rule made it impossible to accept any jobs outside of *Hair* without violating the Equity rule.

Why weren't a lot of the cast fired? It seemed like the most obvious and simple solution. Who knows? Emmeretta Marks was fired at least three times for lateness and absenteeism, then rehired right afterward. That's how it went with many others.

To my knowledge only one assistant director, Danny Sullivan, had the brains to tell the cast that anyone who missed rehearsing his own part at rehearsal would also miss doing it at that night's performance: the rehearsal replacement would go on instead. This worked up to a point. The cast member might stick around for the generally useless rehearsal, but that didn't keep him from doing whatever he felt like onstage and no one in authority would say anything about it.

Although Equity rules permitted only eight hours of rehearsals per week, when you add that to eight shows a week plus the rest of the *Hair* rigamarole (picture calls, publicity gigs, tribal meetings), the show became an all-consuming involvement. As many of the cast tried to maintain some sort of personal life outside *Hair,* more and more began to skip rehearsals altogether, then performances. Lateness and absenteeism were always a problem, but at one point they became the rule rather than the exception. Many of the cast who did show up just screwed around anyway.

The cast was getting worn down. Not from the performances so much as the lack of directorial leadership or control, ego trips on the part of management and the cast, promises about getting it all together, and the total unlikelihood of that ever happening, plus the ever-present "love-tribe" hype. Sometimes I'd ask myself, "What the hell am I doing here knocking myself out?"—especially when I saw the same old people goofing off and taking it easy backstage. But I considered myself a pro, and self-discipline was more important to me than staying away.

After a few months, though, the workhorses began to bitch loudly to the sluffers. Tempers were short. There were arguments. I got an attitude over it, but I really couldn't blame people for not showing. Eventually the other workhorses and I gradually stopped complaining and just withdrew into ourselves. We never really got anything done unless Tom was there.

22

In an attempt to rekindle the aura of love among the tribe, Michael Butler gave a pot luck party at an East Side penthouse for the entire *Hair* company. The idea of "pot luck" at the home of our "millionaire" producer was the cast's. We thought it would be fun if everyone brought a different dish to the party. More like a get-together, it was very relaxed and pleasant. We all enjoyed it.

Then the whole cast was informed at a tribal meeting that the entire *Hair* company was invited to Fire Island for the weekend, Michael Butler's treat. The whole cast and a couple of members of the band were all set to go after a Sunday matinee. No outsiders were allowed, otherwise Elsie Dyson might have driven the bus.

Fred Rheinglas and I had to sweet-talk Elsie into letting Ronnie go along. We promised her we'd take care of her son, that nothing would happen to him. She didn't really want him to go, and if she had known that any part of Fire Island was gay, she never would have let Ronnie on that bus. Somehow Fred and I talked her into it. We got our instructions: "If it's cold, don't let him near the water. Don't let him stay up too late. Make sure he eats right."

All during the lecture Ronnie kept saying, "Mommy, I'll be all right." Otherwise he just sat there with a little "what-can-I-do?" grin on his face.

The bus driver started to rev up the engine.

"Uh-uh, honey, don't you close that door. I'm not ready to get off," Elsie told the driver. Most of us laughed, but he didn't seem to think it was funny.

Crying now, Elsie was still telling us through the bus window to "take care of Ronnie." It was raining like hell. She and her husband followed the bus in their car for about three or four blocks. I didn't know whether to laugh or cry.

Elsie's reputation as a stage mother was only superceded by her reputation as a cook. She had packed us a great meal, much better than the deli-stuff management had provided.

Despite the weather, everyone was very together. There was a lot of joking and laughing. Pot and booze were passed around. The tensions of the show seemed to dwindle with each mile out of the city. That was the purpose of the treat: to keep us close.

It was dark by the time we landed. Someone pointed out our motel, the Boatel. Michael Butler had a suite there. Gerry and Jim were staying elsewhere with friends.

The room Suzannah Norstrand and I shared was very comfortable and not as damp as I thought it would be. There was a dining and dancing area in a smaller building next to the motel. A lot of the cast partied with some of the locals in the bar. Suzannah, Natalie Mosco, who later joined us, and I sat up half the night talking girl-talk.

In another room Jonathan Kramer was freaking out on his first acid trip. He was convinced that Fred Rheinglas was dead. In a panic he woke up Michael Butler to tell him that Fred was dead. They went to Fred's room and found him very much alive.

A few doors away Paul Jabara and Hirem Keller were sharing a room, as we all did. One of the girls in the cast, who was very drunk, ran into their room and crawled under the bed covers between them.

"Hide me, please hide me," she begged. Her old man stormed in right afterwards: "Where is she?" Both Paul and Hiram shrugged. They could feel her cowering beneath them, like a frightened three-year-old. Her old man would have busted their asses if he'd found out they were hiding her.

Apparently, there was a lot of sex play going on. Throughout the rest of the weekend the "Hairy Wonder" (a member of the management) was trying to seduce everyone in sight. One of the guys told me: "I was taking a shower when a member of the staff joined me. 'I really dig you because you're liberated and free,' he said. Then he asked me questions about my personal life. I told him I dug everybody. He asked me if I would help him 'liberate' a friend, also on the staff, who was hung up because he was a closet queen. It was put to me like a challenge so I agreed to go along. The third party was brought into the bedroom and we all rolled around the sack together. I was really surprised that both of the guys were so uptight. Especially with all that 'free love' talk going on."

The next day was sunny and beautiful. Although it was still too cold for me to swim, I went down to the beach. Most of the kids were playing volley ball. Michael Butler was sitting on the beach talking to Erik Robinson, a potential understudy for the part of Claude. Erik, who was from California, had flown in especially to negotiate his contract.

"I was very idealistic and very into knowing where the authors' heads were at," Erik said. "I felt that since I was going to understudy Claude, if I got to know Jim Rado I could take it from there and develop the character on my own."

Erik became very friendly with Gerry and Jim that weekend. They talked a lot, played football, went swimming, and really "got into each other's heads."

Gerry and Jim shared a fenced-off swimming pool where they were staying. When Erik first saw it, there were five or six naked people hanging around, swimming or sunning themselves. Nobody seemed to think anything of it. "I was turned on even more because I thought it exhibited a kind of freedom, especially the kind propagated in *Hair*. Since then I have learned things about Fire Island which make all this sound like *Rebecca of Sunny Brook Farm*."

Another thing that struck him was that some of the people were cast and some were staff but, "Everybody mingled freely and it all seemed like one big happy family. There seemed to be no barriers or class distinction."

Erik thought he was in Paradise. There were lots

of drugs floating around, and although he wasn't into them, it just seemed to be part of the idyll.

"I was invited to orgies that weekend, but, for the most part, I didn't go. When sex happens spontaneously between three or more people who dig each other, when it's natural, that's fine. When invitations are sent out, that turns me off.

"Throughout the weekend, there were certain actions and liberties taken by some of the staff which indicated an ultimatum—do this or else. It was all very subtle, or so it seemed. I wasn't that familiar with the New York theater scene.

"One guy in the staff was interested in me, but the feeling was not mutual as far as sex was concerned. I liked him, but I said, 'No, thanks. It won't work out.'

"Then I discovered that he was the one I had to deal with when it came down to signing my contract. It was beyond me, his position didn't necessarily warrant it. How he got the power, I don't know. Ultimately, I was offered a contract which didn't state in any way, shape, or form that I was to understudy Claude. I had been told by the producer and authors that to understudy Claude was what they wanted me for. I later found out that another guy, who was in fact cooperating with this staff member, had also been promised the exact same understudy part as me. He was given a contract to this effect. He got the part.

"I was upset when I saw the contract. I said as far as I was concerned he [the staff member] could roll the contract into a tube and shove it where he needed it."

Our second night on Fire Island, we were all invited to a party at the home of one of the guys who owned Boatel.

It was held in a large, modern ocean-front house in the Pines. Sally Eaton had come to Fire Island and the party with her baby. When I went upstairs to the john I found them sitting on the floor. Sally was holding the infant's face and calmly blowing pot smoke into it. I just walked away, because I didn't want another confrontation with her over that baby.

Sally used to bring the baby to the theater and lock him in her dressing room. When the baby wasn't locked up, one of the *Hair* groupies took care of him backstage. Most of the time the baby was allowed to crawl around on the filthy floors. I once caught him just as he was about to crawl down a flight of stairs. Many times he was nearly trampled by people running to and from cues.

Almost the whole cast was bugged over Sally's treatment of the baby, but trying to tell her anything about the baby's welfare was useless. After many complaints, she was advised not to bring the baby to the theater. Undaunted, she would sometimes get babysitters to watch him in the alley outside the theater.

She claims that someone reported her to the Society for the Prevention of Cruelty to Children. She accused me and a few others of making the call. I'd never thought of it, but I was glad someone else had.

Despite the incidents of "couch-casting" on Fire Island, balling for Broadway was the least controversial aspect of *Hair*.

One member of the original cast, whom everyone called "The Face," would come right out and tell you that not all of his talent was reserved for the stage. He didn't bullshit. He knew exactly what was happening.

Another common denominator for the original cast,

aside from inexperience, was that, in Erroll Addison Booker's words, "They were slick as far as the street was concerned. They knew how to scheme, how to deal."

When "The Face" left the show, not too long after we opened, no one was surprised that it was to take one of the lead parts in a foreign movie. I asked him how he had gotten the part: "I could tell you, but I don't have to write it out for you."

"I learned that if you fucked to get it, you had to fuck to keep it," Erroll said. "I really didn't want a career lying on my back."

23

There was a fever of TV and radio talk-show appearances following our opening—David Susskind, Johnny Carson, Dick Cavett, Joe Franklin, and later, Ed Sullivan, *Soul,* and the 1969 Tony Awards. I appeared with some or all of the cast on all of them, except for three shows on which I soloed.

In anticipation of the talk shows, Paul Jabara told me excitedly about all his plans for ad-libbing during the "Abie Baby" number. It's one thing to be funny on your own time and another to steal someone else's focus. The "Abe Lincoln" scene was my thing.

"I don't know when you plan on ad-libbing exactly," I told Paul, "but if you try to upstage me during my scene I'll kick your ass from coast to coast on TV."

"Really, Miss Davis!" Paul said, but he apparently took me at my word. On camera he was meek as a lamb. Paul and I once did a closed-circuit TV show together. We talked about *Hair*, naturally, and kept referring to a "Rhonda" and "Rita" in the cast. They were nicknames for two guys in the show, but nobody ever knew the difference.

Hair and I got on the David Susskind show by accident. An agent from Talent Associates had wanted to see me about another job. While I was being interviewed in his office, David Susskind happened to walk by. The agent introduced me as a member of the cast of *Hair*. In those days that never failed to get a response. Mr. Susskind immediately drilled me with questions: "Do you enjoy it?, Do you like the people?, What do you do exactly?", and so on. The hardest one to answer was the one most often asked: "What's it like?"

I wasn't aware enough to talk about what was really happening in *Hair* at the time. I suppose I wasn't ready to face it yet. But the question got me thinking.

"Come around to my office after you finish here," David Susskind said. His office was very plush, full of leather, polished wood, and a panoramic view of the city. I found him easy to talk to, and the outcome was an appearance on his show.

Sally Eaton, Gerry Ragni, Jim Rado, Tom O'Horgan, Michael Butler, and I went on together. For some reason, I felt intimidated by the *Hair* group. Michael was doing his "chief of the tribe" number. Tom O'Horgan was himself. So was everybody else, only more low-keyed. Still, I got the feeling I was being checked, as if I couldn't say exactly what I wanted. I felt that because of my outspokenness, the others were alert to what I *might* say and were on their guard. But the show went smoothly, with no surprises from yours truly.

When I was a nurse I often stayed up late just to see the Johnny Carson Show. Even my mother, who was a sports fan, crazy about wrestling and the Dodgers, liked him.

The first time I ever saw Michael Butler, he was giving a polo exhibition on the Carson Show. He looked very tall on the screen, but next to Johnny Carson he appeared formal and stiff. When the cast was told we had a spot on the Carson Show, I had never connected the polo-playing Butler with the "chief of the tribe." And now we were going to appear on the Johnny Carson Show.

While Michael, Gerry, and Jim discussed *Hair* with Johnny Carson, the cast waited edgily backstage. Finally, our cue. We opened with the slow-motion number, just like at the theater. We were knocking ourselves out to make it good. I noticed many of the cast were knocking themselves out to make themselves look good, too. Some were acting more pushy than usual, trying to get in front-camera positions.

The audience loved the performance. At the end, when some of the cast went out to engage them in clapping and singing, Elsie Dyson was the first to lead the brigade of groupies onstage. Paul and I, who had been told to involve Johnny Carson with the stage action, got him to join us. He took it very well; he went along with our antics, laughed a lot, and acted as though he really dug it. We loved him. He seemed amazed at the energy and vitality of the group: we had another performance to do after his show.

On our way back to the Biltmore, we all felt good.

The vibrations between management and cast were absolutely harmonious. For that moment, the love was true.

Around 47th Street, we bumped into the one member of the cast who didn't make it to the Johnny Carson Show, Emmeretta Marks. She was furious with herself.

"I forgot!" she yelled, skyward. "I forgot!"

The Ed Sullivan Show, on the other hand, was a big down to me and most of the cast. We were appearing with the Lennon Sisters and the contrast—clean cut, All-American Apple Pie *vs.* the hippies—created bad vibes in the studio. The studio stagehands, like *Hair*'s, had a Hardhat attitude. I felt that no one really wanted us there, we were merely controversial.

Ed Sullivan turned me off like a "cracker." Although he copped out by not joining in our finale, he invited people from the audience to do so. We were all glad when that show was over.

Dick Cavett seemed somewhat taken aback by us. But, like Johnny Carson, he went along with our clowning like a trouper. At one point during the show, I sat in his lap. He reacted in that abashed Boy Scout manner of his: "Ahh, shucks folks." I thought it was funny.

I made my TV solo-singing debut on Virginia Graham's "Girl Talk." I was nervous, but felt comfortable because her show took place in a theater.

When it came time for my solo, I really got myself together. I got very caught up in the words and music of a song called "God Bless the Child." My eyes were watering when I finished. A recording offer came out of that appearance. It was from an independent California production company. I thought about it but turned it down. It wasn't really my thing. I wanted to be on the stage.

When Paul Jabara soloed on the Merv Griffin Show, another guest, a guy who seems to be little more than a professional TV panelist, and who is known for his put-downs, had put Paul and *Hair* down so badly that Paul said he was on the verge of tears.

"He put me on the spot. He made me so uptight," Paul later told me.

To Mr. Put-Down that night Paul said, "If Lorrie Davis was here you wouldn't get away with talking like that."

When Merv asked who Lorrie Davis was, Paul explained that I was a cast member. Merv said he'd like to have me on the show sometime. Paul figured I could out-talk Mr. Put-Down, or certainly that I wouldn't take anything from him.

One of Merv Griffin's staff, who bore an uncanny resemblance to Jesus Christ, called me for an interview. I told him that I'd love to do the show. The day they called me I didn't have enough time to get my music together, so I went on and didn't sing.

Bishop Pike, Anna Moffo, and a comedian were also scheduled to appear the day I went on. When I realized Anna Moffo would be singing, I was twice as glad I wasn't. After the perfunctory greetings, Merv asked a few preliminary questions, then slid right into the nitty gritty. Would I be willing to come back on his show with Mr. Put-Down? I had already been asked that question before; I said I'd be glad to appear with anybody.

Merv started rehearsing Mr. Put-Down's opinion of *Hair*. Many of my answers were bleeped out. In response to Merv's saying that Mr. Put-Down walked out on *Hair* before the nude scene, I replied, "He probably walked out because the boys weren't his type." That was cut. The audience loved it. Merv seemed a little uptight over my responses.

I was invited back to do the show two more times. The first time I returned they ran out of time; the last time, a case of laryngitis forced me to cancel. Three strikes and you're out.

Throughout my twenty-five months with *Hair* I was never propositioned by anyone from the audience. I didn't exactly play "Abie" as a come-on to any potential stage-door johnnies out there.

However, after appearing on the Merv Griffin Show I got a call on my answering service from a Mr. So & So. Thinking it was a job offer, I immediately returned the call.

Mr. So & So didn't waste any time getting to the point. He was a wealthy Wall Street stockbroker. He had heard me say on Merv Griffin's show that I didn't have a steady boyfriend. He thought I was beautiful. A girl like me shouldn't have to work. I should have somebody taking care of me, preferably him. He would give me everything I wanted. I wouldn't have to see him all the time, just once or twice a week. He'd help me pick out a new apartment, he'd help me with my career. He had connections. Would I like to have lunch with him to meet and talk it over?

I was flabbergasted. The lunch offer was very tempting, but I knew better.

"Let me think about it," I said after thanking him. "If I'm interested, I'll call you." There seemed to be no cause to trash him. In a way I was flattered, but the whole idea of being "kept" turns me right off. What I'm working for is freedom.

It seemed that everybody wanted a piece of us. We were bombarded with invitations—to previews, parties, openings, premieres, movie screenings, benefits, conventions, fashion shows, protests—for publicity, for free, and for occasional profit.

My spare time was spent doing some or all of the above.

For a while it seemed to be the rage among the "beautiful people" to Invite-A-*Hair*-Cast-Member-To-Your-Party. We partied everywhere from Long Island mansions to private houses on Fire Island to Manhattan penthouses. Most of the parties were dull, boring, and plastic. We were usually the only "hippies" in the room. Everything always seemed forced to me, including us. One welcome exception was a party for James Earl Jones, who I thought gave one of the strongest performances I have ever seen in *The Great White Hope*. I had to tell him so, and did.

Picture calls, with few exceptions, were the biggest drag. Even before we opened there were always a handful of photographers running around taking our pictures. Dagmar, the company photographer, took shots of us while we were still rehearsing at the Variety Arts. She was one of the few female photographers that I saw during my entire run with the show.

After opening night, picture calls became nearly as routine, and just as tiresome, as rehearsals, mainly because they were unbearably chaotic. Dead on our feet after performing one or two shows, we would hang around the theater waiting until two in the morning or later for a photographer, who often never showed up. They tried to pacify us with Chicken Delight until the photographers did show; then they would usually take one shot which didn't include you anyway, but no one could leave without permission. Two exceptions to this were picture calls with photographers Richard Avedon and Ken Duncan. Both were highly organized.

After about a year, most of the kids said "fuck it" and walked out. Some kind of scheduling for picture calls would have been asking for the sun; we already had the moon and the stars.

Next were the hotel gigs. These were mostly hotel convention luncheons or dinners at which members of the *Hair* cast were asked to entertain. We went, sang a few songs, got paid anywhere from $50 to $100 apiece and left. That's pretty high-priced talent for a half-hour's work.

While they sat over their roast beef-chicken dinner plates, we gave them a mini-*Hair* show. We goofed on them as much as they goofed on us. I often felt we were asked as "freaks" more than entertainers. Jonathan Kramer once said the show should have been called *Freaks*. At least we gave the convention crowds something to talk about when they went back home.

Melba, one or two others, George Tipton, and I did a few hotel gigs together. Once we did a free publicity gig for *Hair* for *Life* magazine's 1968 annual party.

Afterwards we were introduced to members of the audience, which was spotted with celebrities. Janis Joplin was there and a couple of astronauts who were so pasty-faced, they struck me as being ill. Maybe the spacemen were spaced out!

24

My sisters Laura and Rita went to see *Hair*. They liked me in it, but they were surprised and confused by some of the material. They made no comments about the show in general, except to say they dug the music. I think they were so busy watching me that they missed half of it.

My eight-year-old neice Norma Jean, one of Laura's children, wanted to see the show. Laura kept hesitating, because of the nude scene and some of the four-letter words. I felt that Norma Jean was bright enough to handle it; she would absorb what she wanted to. What was portrayed on that stage was happening in the streets. Finally, Laura gave in.

Norma Jean sat backstage and watched the entire show like a perfect lady. In fact, the cast loved her. During intermission I took her up to my dressing room. She was very impressed with the whole backstage atmosphere. I think she was getting a touch of stage fever. At the end of Act II, I brought her onstage to dance with the cast, which she loved.

Up in my dressing room after the show, I asked her how she liked it.

"You were fabulous, Aunt Mary," Norma Jean said, "but I loved those two guys, Berger and Woof." (Gerry Ragni and Steve Curry) She wanted to meet them, but was a little shy. She thought Gerry was "funny" in a "crazy" way with his long, curly, red hair, and Steve was "cute." When I finally introduced them to her she blushed and became speechless, which was unusual for Norma Jean.

I asked her if there was anything in the show she wanted me to explain.

"Nope."

Norma Jean never mentioned the nude scene, which she watched quietly and which most adults couldn't stop talking about. In fact, there was a group called Operation Yorkville, which organized itself especially to complain to Mayor Lindsay (to no avail) about the nudity. Nor did Norma Jean say anything about the use of obscene language. She was not used to either nudity or cursing, but the less mysterious and secretive you try to make something for children, the less appealing it becomes to them.

A day or two after Norma Jean had seen *Hair*, Laura told me that she heard her humming the music to "Sodomy," which was Steve Curry's song in the show.

My sister Gloria never saw *Hair*, but to give you an example of our mother's moral influence, here is my twin sister Martha's reaction to *Hair*, before she saw it.

When Martha heard that *Hair* was a hit, she was very happy for me. She carried on about what a great opportunity it was for me to try other things in the theater. The whole time I got the feeling that she wanted to ask me something else about the play. She rattled on a bit more until it finally came out.

"I heard there were people who were *naked* in that show. But I *know* you didn't do it."

I didn't say a word. She continued to talk about this and that, always inserting a comment about the nude scene somewhere. I still didn't say a word. At long last she came right out and asked: "You didn't do that *nude* scene, did you?"

It only took her about two hours to get there. I had to laugh, but very somberly said, "I don't always do it, but I have done it."

"How could you do it?" Martha asked me over and over again. I couldn't explain it to her; she never would have understood.

Martha reacted just like my mother would have, that is, if my mother would have spoken to me at all. I think Moma never would have approved of *Hair*.

25

As *Hair* made headlines, more and more people who were headliners themselves came to see it.

Reportedly, Richard Rodgers considered it "one-third music." He could "hear only the beat." Burt Bacharach thought it didn't even "belong on the same record player with Richard Rodger's music." Leonard Bernstein commented, "the songs are just laundry lists" and walked out.

"Dave Merrick came to see *Hair* during previews and walked out after the first act," Tom O'Horgan said. "The next morning I received a script from him. It was written by Neil Simon. I read two or three pages, said 'it's very interesting, obviously going to be a big show,' but I could see nothing in it I'd be interested in. I sent it back. It turned out to be *Promises, Promises*.

If the audience gives you good vibes, the show is going to be good. One of the best performances we ever gave was the day Janis Joplin was in the audience.

We all knew she was there, sitting with a group of people in about the fourth row orchestra. Janis and her friends were happy and high, passing around joints, applauding, laughing, even speaking to us during a few scenes. We all really dug it. I don't know how much her presence had to do with it, but it was not one of those prove-it-to-me audience nights.

I didn't know Carol Channing was in the audience until I saw her backstage afterwards. In her big booming voice she complimented me on my performance.

At other times I spotted Dianne Carroll, Stevie Wonder, Candy Darling, and the Fifth Dimension, but of all the famous faces in the audience, only one caused me to do a double-take. Distributing flowers during the early part of the Be-In, I looked straight into the face of Peter Lawford, who was about to take a flower. I froze. He was the most handsome man in the house. I kept my eye on him from the stage for the rest of the show.

Robert I. Rubinsky used to roam around the audience during the pre-opening act pretending that he was meditating with a brick. On one particular night, right before the vamp for the slow-motion number, Robert I. pinned Zsa Zsa Gabor in the audience. Still acting like he was freaking out on this brick, he handed it to Zsa Zsa, saying, "This is for you." She looked at it, then at him, and asked in her Hungarian goulash voice, "But darling, vhat am I going to do vith a brick?"

"Build yourself a house," Robert I. stage-whispered.

Many people who came to see *Hair* seemed to forget that it was only a play. There was too much publicity attached to it. Sometimes it was hard to tell the audience from the cast. Were they spectators? Or participants in some crazy, recurring happening?

The people in the audience *Hair* really got to were the ones who left the show or caused a commotion. I thought I knew what uptight meant until I saw some of their behavior. At one point in the show, Berger, played this night by Gerry, descends into the audience to tease them. Gerry's physical appearance and manner is even wilder onstage than off; he would strip down to his jockstrap, and, of course, his body was beautiful.

This particular night he headed for a woman, fortyish, who started to panic when she saw him coming.

"No! No!" she shouted repeatedly as he approached her. By the time he had reached her seat, she was scrambling over the legs of people in her row, hysterically pleading, "Don't touch me! Get away from me!" She really freaked. The rest of the theater passively watched until Gerry calmed her down and got her back to her seat. The woman remained for the rest of the show; Gerry even got her to come onstage during the finale. Later she admitted that the "character" frightened her, but outside of that she loved the show.

In the beginning, the scene that caused more outburst

than any other was the "Don't Put It Down" number, which consisted of three guys who folded the American flag, while singing about how much they dug it. At one point, one of them even cradled and rocked in it. During this scene, some people would storm out of the theater; some booed from their seats until the end of the song; others shouted epithets like, "Reds!" "Commies!" "Shame! Defacing the American flag!," and "If you don't like this country, leave!," as though patriotism began and ended with a piece of colored cloth.

One night a man lost all control. He began screaming about how his son had died in the Army, "defending the flag." Another time, two gray-flannel-suit types started yelling incoherently at us. We couldn't understand a word they were saying. They dramatically exited the theater by burning their ticket stubs in the lobby.

On two separate occasions, spaced two years apart, two different sets of astronauts split over the flag scene. The first astronauts came to see the show soon after it opened. Throughout the first act they seemed to be enjoying themselves. After the flag scene their seats were empty.

Then I later read that Astronauts James A. Lovell, Jr. and John L. Swigert, Jr. repeated the same action in June of 1970. It was the American thing to do. In fact, so American that no one who got riled over the flag scene, including the astronauts, ever realized that the flag onstage was not a flag at all, but a bunting—a piece of cloth in the colors of the national flag used for patriotic or festive decorations. Whoever saw an official American flag with yellow fringe around it?

The second most explosive scene was the Supreme's number, preceded by three white girls singing about their love for "Black Boys." I think more people left the theater en masse during that scene than any other. Since the white girls sang first, by the time we blacks came on it was more than some people could take.

During one particular show, I noticed two entire rows of people, who, up to that point, were obviously enjoying the show, get up and march out. I couldn't hear their remarks but the look of disgust on their faces said it all.

One night it was rumored that Martha and the Vandellas and the real Supremes were in the audience. Allegedly, everyone dug the "White Boys" number with the exception of Diana Ross, the lead singer of the Supremes, who was not too pleased.

There is a scene when a "tourist" couple, a man and his wife, usually played by two white guys, emerges from the audience and goes up onstage. The wife pretends to bump into a black cast member, then makes a remark to her husband about "local color." During one particular performance, Charles O. Lynch (white) was playing the wife and Erroll Addison Booker (black), the husband.

Suddenly, a young man, apparently white, dressed in a sports jacket, came running onto the stage. He was incensed over the wife's remark about "local color" and was yelling to Erroll: "How can you let her say that to you? These people are using you and making fun of you. It's bad enough when white people make fun of black, but when blacks make fun of each other . . ."

"Everybody, except for two or three people onstage, froze," Charles said, "which says something about *Hair*. The cast can relate to people in the audience because they're at an advantage, but when the cast is put at a disadvantage by the audience, it's another thing."

Until the guy from the audience came onstage, it never dawned on Charles that Erroll was black: "When I'm in the show I don't think black or white. I never think of color," he said. Apparently, right after the "local color" remark, Ronnie Dyson, who was standing nearby, said, "Well, how about . . . ?" pointing to Erroll. Suddenly, it dawned on Charles that Erroll was black, and he quickly turned to him ad-libbing, "Oh, honey, I didn't mean you!"

Almost instantaneously, the angry white appeared onstage. While he gave a long harangue on racism, Charles attempted to reassure him that the line was just a part of the play. Finally he said, "Sweetheart, if you don't leave, I'm going to hit you with my pocketbook." Still unaware that Charles was a man in drag, the guy left the stage scowling at everyone and mumbling to himself. There were ushers waiting in the wings to escort him out of the theater.

The incident must have upset Glen Neilson, the assistant director, for after congratulating Charles on the way he handled the situation, he told him that Erroll should never play the role of the husband again.

"That's ridiculous," Charles answered. "There's a once in a lifetime chance it will ever happen again."

As far as I know, it never did, but miscegenation was just another aspect of *Hair* that folks had a hard time swallowing. It was like we were "digging away and eating away at the old things," Tom O'Horgan said, trying to keep changing them. "If you can get any of the blue-haired ladies in the audience turned on to any degree, even a little bit, you've done something."

That the audience was responsive to the show, one way or another, is undeniable. But what was even worse than the nuts, the boos, the hissing, and the hasty exits was a totally silent and hostile audience, one that didn't know how to respond, one like the audience on opening night. When we got one of those, we couldn't do anything right. The bad vibrations coming up over the footlights were really unnerving. I never did a nude scene on a night like that. No reaction was the worst treatment of all.

26

A well-known English actor once asked a member of the cast, "Is it true that all the members of *Hair* have to take drugs to perform?"

The cast member told him that some did and some didn't, but if they did it was because they had to do the show "night after night after night. . . ."

Sally Eaton said that at one time or another more than 75 percent of the cast was heavily into drugs. I could see that it was true of more than half. "Our [Good Doctor] is indirectly responsible for turning the cast into a bunch of junkies," Jonathan Kramer admitted. Most of them got it on with a little bit of help from the doctor. He was even on hand, giving out shots to the cast, during our recording session of the original Broadway score for RCA. And after he stopped coming to see us, some of us would go see him.

Some claimed they couldn't do the show without their

"vitamins." One guy said that, at first, he thought the only way he could play Berger was "on speed." Paul Jabara told me that "they made us feel it was groovy, that we were in, groovy, and hip to do the show on drugs, especially mescaline and acid. It got to the point where the Good Doctor was going to start his own world. If you were part of his cosmic universe it was really something." He admitted that doing the show straight was much better, even when exhausted. "I got crazy on speed."

One of the guys in the show, who was a swinger—someone who fills in for three or four parts—got his one and only shot without even asking for it. One night he accidentally hurt his knee during a performance and fell flat on his face. He was carried backstage in real pain, although he was trying to be cool about it. Suddenly, the Good Doctor was standing over him, hypo poised, about to give him a shot. I asked him what was in the shot.

"It's a calcium shot," he said.

"What does he need that for?"

The doctor mumbled about how good it would be for him and socked the stuff into his muscle. The house physician's assistant, who showed up later, asked to see the bottle, but the Good Doctor wouldn't show it to him. The swinger later told me that the next thing he knew, he was hanging from the ceiling, floating like a cloud. He was stoned until six o'clock the next day. Admittedly, he dug it, but "if you're not careful you could freak."

The next day another guy in the cast took him to the Good Doctor's office to have his leg treated. He said he sat for two hours waiting while The Man gave shots to a bunch of people who were hanging around the office. Apparently, "they were really in trouble. They had to have it."

Robert I. said he took the shots "because they were for free."

Erroll Booker, who had been hanging around with the *Hair* crowd, admitted that he started taking the Good Doctor's shots before he entered the show. "I was into drugs and that whole peace and love thing then." After he joined the show he started taking barbiturates. "I quit smoking grass because I got so paranoid from the pressures around the theater." He used to down six or seven "downs" a day with a cup of whiskey.

"There were two very conflicting things happening. One was the show, which we were all trying to believe in, and the other was the real world. . . ."

Instead of taking fewer drugs, everyone started taking more and more as the show wore on. "The longer the show was running, the more depressed we got," Paul Jabara said. "We would take on each other and more drugs. Before you knew it, people were into heavy stuff."

One girl, who was in the Off-Broadway *Hair*—"Very few kids in that show were on drugs."—started getting down because she saw things happening to people around her who least deserved it, and after two and a half years nothing was happening to her. She got more and more strung out on drugs.

"Once your nerves are frazzled with speed, you need something to calm yourself down," Jonathan Kramer said. "In 1968 and 1969, President Nixon waged a war on pot and created a pot famine. All you could get was skag [heroin]. A lot of people started sniffing skag, and some couldn't perform without it."

The first time Erroll Addison Booker ever took skag was while he was in *Hair*. He didn't get into it heavily until after he left the show. "Dr. Gilbert [the house physician] had given me an antibiotic shot for a bad cold. A cast member said, 'Come into the john. I have something for you.' A lot of kids were into skag then." Allegedly, so were some members of the band and a few people in management.

Some of the kids thought it was kicky to do the show on acid. "I wouldn't care to do the show going up on acid," Sally Eaton told me, "but I did it once coming down after our last trip to Fire Island" (we subsequently had two more trips). "I had been tripping and was still tripping when we returned. It was a new perspective on the show. I saw a lot of things in the part of Jeanie I had missed before. I kept looking out into the audience and seeing the dunes of Fire Island."

Doing the show stoned on one thing or another just became part of the gig for most. One night it was hash brownies.

Before a performance one night, a guy in the cast handed out a plate of hash brownies. Except for one girl, most of the cast who ate them got through their performances without any trouble. She was usually so spaced out that most of the time she could never finish the show, if she could ever begin it in the first place. Rumor had it that someone in management had kept her in the show, because otherwise there was no explanation for what she got away with onstage. Whatever the rest of us were doing, she was doing the opposite. Whether it was blocking, dialogue, singing, or dancing, she was always out of whack. She would cover other people's lines, making up her own, move wherever she wanted, and just goof off in general. Once in a while she'd give a good straight performance.

Straight performances were the exception rather

than the rule. One time Jonathan Kramer was singing "My Conviction," and something about as big as a marble fell out of his nose. He finished the song, then swooped it up with a handkerchief. "I took it home, chopped it up, and sniffed it right back up again. It was an accumulation of 'junk.' That's how poor I was in those days."

Another time, Robert I., bored, broke a popper (amyl nitrate) on stage while everybody was singing "Hair." He and Jonathan sniffed it. Someone finked to the stage manager and they got fired for it. "I got fired once every three hundred performances," Jonathan said. "Julie Arenal always brought me back. In the end I had to get out of the country to get it together.

"When I went back in October 1971, it looked like it was snowing backstage, so much white powder was floating around."

The capper to all this was the no-dope rule in the theater. At one of our first tribal meetings, Michael Butler—he sitting onstage, we in the audience—lectured us somberly about smoking pot in the theater.

It was against the law, he said, and the show could be closed because of it. There would be no third warning, he said. Any violators would be released from the show without any further discussion. Jonathan Kramer walked out mid-lecture: "I couldn't stand the hypocrisy." It was no big secret that many of the staff smoked pot, or did worse, including some in top management. The no-dope rule became a sick joke backstage.

Actually, we weren't supposed to smoke *anything* backstage. Every once in a while a fire department inspector would pay us a surprise visit. When the man in the red hat came, the stage manager of the moment would yell repeatedly into the loudspeaker, "Marti Whitehead, would you please come to the desk." This was a warning for everybody to snuff their butts. Marti Whitehead was the name of some girl who had left the show. I used to hear her name a lot and always wondered what the constant chatter about "Marti Whitehead" was all about.

27

Money was always a sore subject with the cast. The majority of us were being paid minimum chorus wages ($130), but there was really no chorus in *Hair*. The chorus became a principal role in the show; it was us, and we were the show. As people got careless and began leaving their check stubs on tables, we found out that some of us were making more than others. Ronnie Dyson was making more, but he deserved it. For me, it wasn't a matter of who was making what so much as getting what you deserved for the amount of work you put in.

Most of us felt cheated.

Three days after opening night, Standing Room Only tickets were being sold. The house capacity was 1600. After the first month we all asked for more money.

CAST: We'd like more money.
MANAGEMENT: We aren't making any.
CAST: What do you mean?
MANAGEMENT: There's no money.
CAST: What do you mean?
MANAGEMENT: There's expenses, blah, blah, blah.

There was a credibility gap somewhere. Rumors about who did less and made more than those who did more and got less circulated backstage. I decided to ask for a raise. I felt I deserved it.

I went to Victor Samrock, the business manager. He told me the show wasn't making any money, but raises would be forthcoming as soon as it was. I said O.K., but the more S.R.O. crowds I saw straining to see the show, the more annoyed I became. The who-made-what rumors got thicker backstage.

Then one day we were informed of a pending Actor's Equity strike. Equity was trying to raise the minimum wage, so there would be no raises until the strike was settled.

A girl in the *Hair* office told me that Michael Butler didn't vote to strike. On June 17, all the Broadway shows closed down. There was an onslaught of tribal meetings in Michael Butler's office-wigwam around that time.

The *Hair* business office was located in the West Fifties. It was in an old, rundown building, a walk-up. The P.R. flak sheets referred to the office as a "stage set for an eighth-rate impresario who has, after a generation of trying, at last failed to make the rent." It was supposed to be "another study in contrast. . . ." To the people who worked there, it was a horror show.

According to the girl in the *Hair* office: "We'd say, 'Listen, we found this great office space. You have to take the elevator to the fourth floor . . .'

"Michael would say, 'No.'

"Meanwhile, we'd be fighting the rats. It's not his fault that there were rats, but there they were. All summer, while we were working at the desks, it was nothing for a rat to walk or run down the middle of the floor. Great big enormous ones. If you had to work late, forget it. They were all over the place. You screamed, they ran. And you kept your feet up for the rest of the day. We kept on trying to find a new office.

"In the beginning Michael used to come to the office, lie down on the couch, and play records full blast. He'd eat Clark bars and sign necessary papers. He was a great boss. He never bothered with or talked to anyone unless they talked to him. He's very shy in a way.

"People arrived between ten and eleven in the morning. The staff was never there half the time. People would cover for each other. The place was a shambles. Some of us used to trip out ɔn THC in the afternoons while trying to work.

"If Michael missed a phone call, or something of importance, then it was bad. That affected him personally. When the other companies started opening, beginning with Los Angeles, he started pulling himself together. There was a big crackdown."

Eventually, as *Hair* expanded around the globe, the office moved to a new building. Management seemed to concentrate less on "a Phoenix rising out of its own ashes," and more on efficiency. The new office was in an elevator building with a glass-partitioned reception area.

Meanwhile, in the old office, where the "American theater was still being re-born," Michael Butler sat behind his slightly elevated desk and did his "chief of the tribe" thing with us. After we had been told about the proposed Equity strike, he explained the *Hair* money-lending fund. The cast could borrow money from the company and pay it back after we returned to work. I thought it was a nice gesture. A lot of the cast really needed the money, and most of us borrowed.

A tribal meeting or two later, Michael hit us with his *Hair*-In-The-Streets idea. He wanted to put on a kind of wandering *Hair* exhibition for kids in the slums. The plan was to decorate and repaint a truck to look like the *Hair* stage set, then take it all over the poorer sections of the city for free performances.

We all liked the idea, but the strike, which only lasted a few days, ended before we could get it on. Then we decided to go ahead with it anyway, for half a day's pay, on Sundays, but nothing ever came of it. In time, the cast just lost interest. During the strike, relationships between management and cast improved. We were all going to sink or swim together again.

After the Equity representative saw the show, we were informed we should have been paid for all the *extra* parts and singing roles we did. Most of us were not even aware we were doing "extras" until we started receiving retroactive checks for them. When the Equity strike was settled, all those making minimum wages were brought up to the new minimum: $145 immediately and $155 over three years. Nevertheless, I still felt I deserved more.

I put off asking for a raise for a while, because of the minimum-wage raise plus the "extra" parts pay. Many in the cast were afraid to ask for raises because they didn't want to be fired. But the more I thought about the paycheck of a girl who carried much less weight in the show than I, but got paid more, the angrier I became. Then I noticed that some kids got billing who weren't doing shit in the show. One day I decided, "This is it." Nothing else mattered—I didn't want to quit, but I would have to if they didn't pay me more. I called my sister Laura and told her what was what. She said, "If you don't think they're treating you fairly you have no choice."

Getting the cast ready to play *Hair* was weirder than the play itself. Tom O'Horgan, our director, put us through Sensitivity Exercises like the breathing exercise *(above)* — by learning to breathe as one we learned to feel as one. *From left to right:* Donnie Burks, Margi LiPari, Leata Galloway, Lamont Washington, Emmeretta Marks. The exercises developed into the actual staging of scenes; learning to move as one *(below)* became an important part of the Be-In and other numbers. Lynn Kellogg, Jim Rado and Natalie Mosco form a chain over Donnie Burks and Lamont Washington.

Rehearsal: Galt MacDermot, *Hair*'s composer, taking an infrequent break *(left)*; Melba Moore and I singing his score (You'd think I could read—music, that is.). *Below:* Robert I. Rubinsky winces at my caress in an early version of The Tourist Couple, as Jonathan Kramer, the Tourist "Lady," makes up to Ronnie Dyson. In back row: Leata Galloway, Lamont Washington, Walter Harris (in flag).

Leaders of the Tribe: Tom O'Horgan and Julie Arenal in a rare moment. *Left below*: The Chief. *Right below*: The authors Jim Rado *(left)* and Gerry Ragni (What a hunk of man!) backstage at the Biltmore getting ready to open the show.

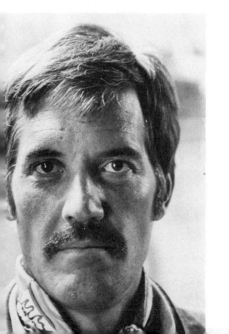

(Top) "Aquarius," the opening scene. Sheila (Lynn Kellog) burns a lock of Claude's (Jim Rado) hair while Berger (Gerry Ragni in loincloth) looks on. *Foreground*: Ronnie Dyson; Margi LiPari is at right.

(Bottom) "I Got Life" was usually a show-stopper. Woof (Steve Curry) holds mike for Claude (Jim Rado) who tells his mother (played in triplicate by: Paul Jabara, Jonathan Kramer, and Sally Eaton) that he, too, has life.

(Opposite) "Hair." Letting it all hang out. *(Back row*: Steve Gamet, Gerry Ragni, Steve Curry and Lynn Kellogg, under blond mop. Margi LiPari, *middle*, wore hers short. *Front row*: Natalie Mosco, Paul Jabara, Jim Rado, Diane Keaton, Suzannah Norstrand. *Foreground*: Shelly Plimpton.)

(Left) A heavy taste of soul—some ten feet above the stage. Emmeretta, Melba and I in one dress sing "White Boys."

(Right) They just don't make shoeshine boys like they used to! Natalie Mosco shines my shoes with her hair as I recite the Gettysburg Address. (That's Paul Jabara trying to upstage me.)

(Opposite, top) Lamont as Hud.

(Opposite, bottom) Paul Jabara *(foreground)* and Ronnie Dyson, at a peace-pipe get-together on Fire Island.

The Tribe. Claude (Jim Rado) lying on stage during his "trip." From left to right standing: Donnie Burks, Margi LiPari, Steve Gamet, Hiram Keller (he's back there), Suzannah Norstrand, Gerry Ragni, Sally Eaton, Walter Harris, Shelly Plimpton, Leata Galloway, Natalie Mosco, Lynn Kellogg, me, Emmeretta Marks and Paul Jabara. Kneeling at left: Diane Keaton.

I called the *Hair* office to make sure Michael Butler was there and made an appointment to see him. Win or lose, I'd try for a raise this time. I waited in the office for a few minutes. I guess Michael could tell from the expression on my face that I wasn't about to take no for an answer. I anticipated a long poverty story. We were both very cordial.

"What do you want to see me about?"

"I'm here because I want a raise."

I waited for the sob story, ready to pounce on him with a rebuttal.

"O.K.," he said. "How much do you want?"

I expected any response but that one. For once I was at a loss for words.

"Is $75 a week enough?" he asked.

You could have knocked me over with a breeze.

Struggling to keep cool, I said, "Yes. That's fine. Thank you."

"Is there anything else I can do for you?"

Not at the moment. I left. A $75 a week raise? I expected $15, maybe $20, a week. The whole thing made me light-headed.

By July 8, all evening performance tickets to *Hair* went up to $11 a seat. Prior to that the weekly break-even point was $34,000. With the new ticket price, weekly income potential was now approximately $60,000 to $68,000.

Michael Butler also had a "scalper-elimination" plan of selling choice orchestra tickets at $50 a seat to big corporations on a subscription basis. As long as he was in show business, he stated in the papers, he wanted to do everything he could to "be helpful." The plan was eventually dropped because there weren't enough takers.

Management tried not to miss a trick. The *Hair* company sold copies of the original Broadway cast record to us, the original Broadway cast, at $1.50 per album. NOT FOR SALE—PROMOTION USE ONLY was stamped in the upper left-hand corner on the back of each one. Most of the kids bought at least three albums each. I bought five or six to give out to family and friends.

When I asked Fred Rheinglas who was getting the money, he just smiled.

Around that time, the "tribe" notified Michael Butler that we wanted to meet with him, particularly about raises, *alone*. We wanted to have a heart to heart talk to try to straighten out a lot of other shit, too. Our message for him to come alone was very specific. The tribal meeting was to be held in the theater balcony. Michael Butler showed up with one of his cronies, Joe Cavallaro.

When I pointed out, somewhat angrily, that we had requested him to come by himself, he didn't bother to reply.

Many of the cast respected Michael Butler, or wanted to, but as long as he hid behind his "clan" or "inner-tribe," he wasn't really in touch with us. He made no real contact. I suddenly flashed on something: a man is only as good as the people he surrounds himself with. There was always a wall of people around Michael Butler. Some of them were no doubt invaluable, but there were others who had jumped on the *Hair* bandwagon.

If Michael Butler couldn't face us alone, then there was no sense in having tribal meetings, or even a tribal chief for that matter. As Melba once said, "One side never knew what the other side thought."

28

On one subject, both sides shared the same concern: the Phantom was raising hell.

Claude's gorilla costume and the Electric Blues costume were found, slashed, in a garbage pail in the alley.

Jonathan Kramer's fur coat and Paul Jabara's new leather coat also had both been slashed.

Some of Paul's clothes and Jonathan's new shoes were found in one of the johns, pissed on.

Lamont Washington's new boots were discovered shit upon in a toilet.

"This has got to stop!" Michael Butler would say at our tribal meetings. We would try to devise ways and means of catching the Phantom: we thought of hiring a full-time security guard, taking fingerprints, even pleading with him: "You're a sick person," and promising to help if he or she would identify himself.

Some kids played detective. They would leave the stage during the show and go upstairs to check around. We would often bump into each other skulking around: "Just checking up on the Phantom." It seemed safer to go Phantom-hunting during a performance, when there were plenty of people onstage and around the theater. We became a cast of paranoids. And after what happened to one guy, I was ready to see someone hanging from the rafters before too long.

Jim Fields came up from Tennessee to take over the part of "Hud" from Donnie Burks. He was very homesick, and there wasn't a person in the theater who didn't know it. He used to talk endlessly about the wonders of Tennessee. Jim had pinned a number of keepsakes and pictures of his family and friends to the wall above his dressing table. Each photograph was marked somewhere—mother, father, grandmother, girlfriend. It was sort of pathetic.

One day someone ran up to me, "Did you hear what happened to Jim Fields' pictures?"

When I found out I knew the Phantom was really demented. Every one of Jim's photographs was hanging in its original place, sliced to ribbons. It looked like the calling card of a twisted mind.

Everybody was angry and upset, including the stagehands and musicians. We all became suspicious of one another. I started to walk around backstage, especially going in and out of dressing rooms, singing loudly. Or I'd yell, "I'm coming in." We all did it. Nobody wanted to ease up on the Phantom; nobody wanted to surprise him or her in the act.

One night Jonathan Kramer was getting ready to do his Margaret Mead number. He had put on his costume—hat, glasses, fur coat, ladies' shoes, stockings, garter belt, and jockey shorts—then grabbed his gloves and had run down to the stage. He was late. While running, he started putting on one of his gloves and noticed something stuck inside. A razor blade had been inserted in one of the fingers. He became hysterical.

Management talked about bringing in security police but nothing substantial ever resulted from either the idea or the action. Allan Nicholls told me, after we had both left the show, that he ran across a cop who told him: "I was one of the cops who investigated the Phantom. We never caught him," the cop said.

Then someone decided to have our handwriting analyzed—another shot in the dark. I was waiting for management to uncover the Phantom astrologically next.

Most of us speculated about who the Phantom could be. It had to be a cast member, not a stagehand, we thought—someone on the perimeter. There were a number of emotionally unstable people in the cast; besides, we were always being pitted against each other. Almost everyone had their own theory about who it was. Some would even openly accuse others, face to face. There were many arguments and fights over it, creating another backstage bitch.

"This has got to stop!" management said.

I got more and more paranoid, especially when I saw the Phantom could anticipate our schemes before they even happened. I began to imagine things for him or her to do: cut the rope Gerry swung on; saw off part of the Supreme's plank, or grease it. I read disaster into every splinter and creak.

Some of the kids would pull mock-Phantom stunts. Paul Jabara told me that he once caught a fly and put it in Jonathan Kramer's orange drink. Another time, he drank Ronnie Dyson's soda—"I was really thirsty."—and left a note saying, "T-H-E P-H-A-N-T-O-M."

But it was no joke. A member of the cast, who was nicknamed "Joey Heatherton," owned a beautiful shirt which was made in Hong Kong. He wore it to the theater frequently. One day the shirt was found cut to pieces.

It was probably the only time the Phantom did something which pleased almost everyone. "Joey" was not the most popular cast member. He would strut around saying, "I have talent. You don't."

Just about everyone was hit by the Phantom, although nothing personal was ever done to me. Very early in the Phantom's game I expressed myself loud and clear at a tribal meeting: "If the Phantom ever does anything to me, and I find out who it is, I'll kick his ass. And if I can't do it, I know somebody else who will." I never had any trouble. One time my Abe Lincoln hat was missing, then later found under the stage. Another time the Supreme's costume was found in some odd place. Maybe it was the Phantom's doing, maybe not.

29

To say that *Hair* had a discipline problem would be like saying, "The American Indian got a raw deal," or, "There is racial unrest in America." From the dressing rooms to the relationship between management and cast to backstage conditions to the actual stage performance, *Hair* made its own rules. Obviously, there were more inequities than Equity could handle.

As things deteriorated backstage, slowly but surely they began to show up onstage. There, the havoc still seemed to the audience just another part of the wild show, but to many in the cast it was one big humiliation.

For example, many of the girls in the cast were onstage only for their specialty numbers, or when they felt like it. Otherwise they would take coffee breaks, pot breaks, sex breaks, rest breaks, or just break-breaks. Often there were more performers in the dressing room than onstage. The habitual break-takers were never openly called down, but if someone like me, who usually could be depended on, left the stage for any reason, she heard about it immediately. I guess they had to throw their weight around somewhere.

If I didn't love being onstage so much I probably would have stayed off, too. I loved doing the show, as did a few of the others, but when we wound up having to cover for someone at the last minute, we got mad. Ordinarily, most performers are told by the stage manager before the performance when they will have to take over someone else's role. Ordinarily, most performers welcome the chance to do more onstage. There was nothing "ordinary" about anything in *Hair*.

The final outrage was not when people missed shows but when they didn't even bother to call in to let anyone know they'd be out. As a result, the stage manager would give you a message, usually via another cast member, minutes before you were to fill in for the absentee. Sometimes the performer himself would say, "I'm going to the john. Say my lines for me." Or someone would ask if they could do your lines for a change. Sometimes you'd be onstage and suddenly realize that someone was missing. Quickly, either you or someone else had to say their lines. If no one noticed who was missing the lines were just skipped. Whoever followed was stuck with improvising his way out.

At one particular performance, everything went fine

until the band played the vamp for the introduction to "Aquarius." It began to seem like an unusually long vamp to me.

During this scene we're supposed to relate to a member of the cast and that night for me it was Sakinah. I mentioned the drawn-out vamp to her. Since she was Ronnie Dyson's understudy, she became alarmed. After I discovered that Ronnie was missing from the stage, I told Sakinah. Now she was incredulous. Nobody had told her to fill in for him.

I hesitated to say anything to the stage manager, because she wasn't getting along with most of the cast. I, too, had had some differences with her. Then I weakened. Telling Sakinah to get ready to sing "Aquarius," I went to inform the stage manager.

Her first reaction was, "Stop fooling around. Get back onstage."

"If you think I'm fooling around, where's Ronnie?" She checked the stage, tried calling him on the house intercom, then finally checked the attendance sheet. Ronnie had never signed in. The whole thing was an oversight. Very embarrassed, she began to panic. "Tell Sakinah to do it." I told her I already had.

We had two shows to do on Christmas day, 1968, and nobody wanted to work at all, let alone do a matinee and an evening performance. The matinee was the worst show I ever was in.

Only two out of the five leads showed up. Five of the chorus were out, too. Some sixteen people, mostly badly rehearsed understudies, were left to carry the show.

The remaining cast members eagerly volunteered to do certain parts, and the stage manager, who should have been used to this by now, acted flustered and went along with the volunteers. I was in a state of dread.

From the first note of "Aquarius," things went wrong, then steadily downhill. Leata Galloway, who had volunteered to fill in for Ronnie Dyson, began singing the song in the wrong key. By the time she found the right one, the chorus came in. When the solo resumed, she couldn't seem to decide whether to sing the song an octave higher or lower. She compromised: some parts were sung higher, some lower. It was so bad that the chorus tried to cover over by joining in parts that were usually sung solo.

Lines and cues and blocking were blown throughout the entire first act. Again, the chorus tried to cover up by saying many of the lead lines just to make sure they were said.

Finally, the Be-In. Robert McNamara, Claude's understudy, sang "Where Do I Go?" sharp and flat. Thankfully the stagelights were low. I was mortified to be a part of this performance. One cast member, Donnie Burks, cried during and after the show.

"At least," I thought, "it can't get any worse."

Three out of the four performers who sang "Electric Blues," in Act II didn't know their parts. They sounded like a bad amateur street-group. By this time, a lot of kids decided to remain offstage, which wasn't unusual, except we were more short-handed than usual.

The performance got so bad that I started imagining the whole experience as a nightmare.

The war scene ran through its usual strobe-lit course, until the part where the nuns, who had just killed the monks, are waiting for the astronauts to come out and do us in. We waited and waited. No astronauts. By the time we realized that none of the astronauts were coming out to kill us, we just died onstage, virtually and figuratively.

One of the most poignant parts of the war scene is

the duet, "What A Piece of Work Is Man," sung by Ronnie Dyson and Walter Harris from a balcony while the casualties of the war scene lie dead on the stage.

Before Leata Galloway and Robert McNamara had finished the song, all of us lying on stage wished we really were dead. Even my elementary school performances were better. Not only did they sing off-key and muck-up the harmony, but they forgot some of the words. The band played to total silence. Desperately, the stage dead were miraculously resurrected and, still lying there, picked up the song and finished singing it for them.

That whole sequence just about finished me. Why people wanted to go on, knowing they were badly rehearsed or unprepared, is a mystery to me. It seemed that nobody, particularly the stage manager, took the initiative to rehearse the understudies.

To make matters worse, a young girl, who had been crouching below the stage for nearly the whole show, came up onstage near the end of Act II, during the "Good Morning Starshine" finale.

Fred Rheinglas motioned to Erroll Addison Booker to get her off the stage. Erroll said he and someone else had tried, but the girl fought them off. "Fuck it," Erroll finally said. "I ain't going to have nothing to do with it. This chick is out of her mind."

This happened just before the cast went out into the audience. Before that I had seen another girl during the war scene and told her to leave the stage because she could get hurt. I even led her off.

When Erroll failed, Fred motioned me to try. I went to grab her arm. "Oh, please let me stay, please let me stay," she begged. Suddenly, Emmeretta Marks came up to us, and pushed me while trying to snatch our hands apart. "Let her go," she said. "Who do you think you are? It's none of your business."

I forgot everything. I asked her who she thought she was pushing. Emmeretta lapsed into a curse bag. I mean she called me everything but a "child of God." Then I lost my temper. The band was playing and the cast was going out into the audience to sing "Good Morning Starshine." A couple of the boys in the cast stepped between us as I went for Emmy and she ran offstage. When we reached the back of the theater I remember attempting to reason with her. She got about one bad word out of her mouth and I hit her.

We got to the back of the house, Erroll said, "and you started whooping, like 'wham!' You jumped back and did your Avenue D number. You put your dukes up and you were whippin' . . ."

I was so totaled by anger that I can't even remember what happened. I do know it cleared the air between Emmeretta and me. After that, things were much better between us.

Unfortunately, I could not say the same for the show. Shortly after the Christmas matinee and evening debacles, I stayed out for a day. It was only my second time in the show, and the first was back in August—for good reason. In both cases, I didn't have the heart to come in.

For all its craziness and backstage bitching, there wasn't too much violence at *Hair,* just occasional fisticuffs between members of the love-tribe who didn't like each other much. Jonathan Kramer and Lamont Washington had got at it very early in the show, so did Paul Jabara and Ronnie Dyson. And Emmeretta Marks and I had our little row.

But one night there was a fight onstage which looked so good under the strobe lights—it happened during the war scene reversal—that the audience applauded. At the time only the cast knew it was for real.

Jim Rado and Linda Compton, so the story goes, had taken off one afternoon, and while she claimed it was all very innocent, they were gone a long time.

Throughout the performance that night, Gerry kept asking Jim and Linda where they had gone and what they had done. Both tried to tell him that nothing had happened—they had just gone to a movie—but Gerry wouldn't give up. By the time we got to the war scene, Gerry was stewing in his own juices. He broke the blocking by jumping over everybody, and attacked Jim.

Jim may have been on something that night, because he absolutely freaked out. He crawled offstage on his hands and knees, screaming like a frightened kid to the stage manager.

Meanwhile, the cast was onstage singing, right before "What A Piece of Work Is Man," "Love, Love . . ."

Jim ran up to dressing room number one. The stage manager, worried, followed and found him huddled in a corner, whimpering. The stage manager tried to comfort him and soothingly talked him back onto the stage. He crawled back onstage.

A member of the cast told me that after the show, Gerry and Jim went to Joe Allen's. The scene was very tense. Afterwards, Jim didn't want Gerry to get into the car with him. Apparently Jim was really scared shitless.

30

With the exception of the vociferous few, most audiences were floored by *Hair*. They just went along with whatever happened. They never seemed to mind when understudies were substituted, or even when substitutes substituted for substitutes. However, there was one particular segment of the audience to whom it did make a difference. The show's best and worst critics, the *Hair* groupies.

Hair groupies differed from the usual autograph hunters, stage-door hounds, and star-struck "paparazzi" who hang around theaters like vultures. Similar to Rock groupies, they differed only because they embraced an entire Broadway Rock musical instead of one Rock superstar or group. They had no official connection with the show, but after a while they were as much a part of it as any of us. In some cases, even more.

The typical New York *Hair* groupie came from white, middle-class backgrounds. Except for one, who was in his twenties, they were all teenaged boys and girls who hung around us day and night. Some had seen the show over two hundred times. Tony Barbato told me that he "never wanted the show to end."

The oldest groupie worked as a ticket seller but confided that he was a frustrated opera singer. By the time I had talked to him he had seen *Hair* a total of 107 times. "The fiftieth time I got a free ticket." He was so well known that a standing-room-only spot was always reserved for him.

One night the cast introduced him to the audience. He had seen the show over a hundred times by then, and it was also his birthday. The audience applauded him, then later the cast gave him a birthday party with candles and cake backstage after the show. He was in Heaven.

His biggest dream was to be in *Hair*. Everyone of the *Hair* groupies had the same fever. None of them seemed to regard the musical as a piece of theater as much as a way of life. "Why couldn't I be in it, too?" they'd ask.

One sixteen-year-old boy, Eddie, said, "There's something that you're saying up there. . . . It's a kind of message. I don't want to be an actor, but I want to do *Hair*." After he saw it for the first time, he went backstage and asked: "How do you get into *Hair*?"

Dennis Erdman, another sixteen-year-old, who had seen the show over 130 times, said that anticipating the nude scene made him nervous, but it was "so sudden and natural," that "before *Hair* I wouldn't think of taking my clothes off at a Be-In. Now I would."

Tony, who had auditioned for *Hair* nine times at the last count, said he wasn't interested in other musicals, only *Hair*. "It was the first musical to come out with the story of my life."

"Eighteen hundred kids auditioned for the San Francisco *Hair*; four thousand for Chicago," Tom O'Horgan said.

"These kids go to audition for *Hair* the same way somebody else might make a religious pilgrimage. These are people with a need to communicate, to have some common cause, to find something which they can really believe in. This is the first time that the meaning of the piece is more important than the thing itself."

Many of the New York *Hair* groupies performed the whole show outside in the alley next to the Biltmore while the kids inside were doing it onstage. Some, I was told, were better than the ones inside.

Many of the *Hair* groupies were used and abused by some members of the cast. A few of the guys in the show made passes at the boys, promising they would help get them into the show if they would sleep with them. To my knowledge none of the groupies I knew ever got into the show. One girl, who'd auditioned many times, said they were encouraged a lot but nothing ever seemed to come of it.

Tony said that most of the kids who were getting into the show, outside of the original cast, were the ones with "experience in and out of bed. Most of them had that type of reputation." Anyway, "you could tell . . . because they had no talent."

The *Hair* groupies fed the egos of the cast by running errands and just catering to the cast in general. Sally Eaton often asked them to baby-sit for her at home or in the theater. Some in the cast enjoyed having the groupies around just to put down. It was a sick head game.

Many of them must have found it trying, because they didn't like discussing it, even two years after. But it seemed that any kind of association with *Hair* was better than none at all. "It was just *the* thing to do," Tony said.

31

On Monday night, August 10, 1968, Donnie Burks, a friend of mine, and I went with Lamont Washington to Steve Paul's *Scene*. Afterwards Lamont wanted us to come back to his place to party, but there was a matinee the following day and I wanted to get some sleep.

A few hours later that night, the phone awakened me. Lamont's manager, Ernestine McClendon, was on the other end, crying uncontrollably. Somehow the message got across: "A fire . . . Lamont leaping from his apartment window . . . in critical condition at St. Vincent's Hospital." Would I tell *Hair* management?

At first I thought Ernestine was kidding. I didn't want to believe what I had heard.

The emergency room at St. Vincent's Hospital confirmed her call. At least fifty percent of Lamont's body was badly burned and he had multiple internal injuries. I knew it was a near-fatal injury. *We should have gone home with him to party*. A couple of hours later I called St. Vincent's again. Only family members were allowed patient information and visiting time.

At ten in the morning I called Fred Rheinglas at his home to tell him. He was as shocked as I. A picture of Lamont, taken just before he jumped, was spread across the front page of the *Daily News*. It was taken by a man, "an amateur photographer," who lived in the same building and had "aimed across the courtyard."

Lamont, apparently looking for a way to escape the fire, jumped two floors from his kitchen window to the roof of an adjacent one-story building. Nobody ever discovered the cause of the fire, but supposedly his mattress caught fire while he was asleep.

The thought, "If we had gone home with him, it never would have happened," nagged me. I was numb from thinking about it.

Lamont lay critically ill in the hospital for fifteen days. Every time any of us called the hospital the message was the same: no visitors except for family. On August 25, 1968, he died.

When the cast was officially informed of his death, we each assumed that we'd attend the funeral. That night Ronnie Dyson and I had dinner with Fred Rheinglas to discuss the possibilities of closing the matinee show the day of the funeral, a Wednesday matinee only two days away, so we all could attend both the funeral and burial.

Up until that moment, Ronnie and I had felt close to Fred. As we were talking, I started picking up on bad vibes. It seemed to me Fred really didn't care that much one way or another about what had happened to Lamont. To even consider closing the show seemed like an annoying obligation to him. Nothing more. His parting words to us were to the effect that they [management] could close the show if they wanted to, but what would we do with the time? So we'd better be at the theater.

"All I have to do is stay black and die," Ronnie said bitterly.

I was determined to pay my respects to Lamont and his family. I was going to attend that funeral and the burial regardless of the consequences. My mind was made up and no one but me could unmake it. I expected every individual in the cast to act according to his own conscience in the end.

In the meantime there were many meetings about whether or not to do the show that Wednesday. Lamont's popularity with the cast was not an issue. As one guy in the cast put it, "Lamont was a force that moved very deliberately to where he was going."

He was a member of the tribe.

Gerry and Jim kept repeating they definitely would not do the show, and they carried on by hugging us and each other and talking up the love thing between the tribe.

On Wednesday almost everybody in the show asked me if I was doing the matinee. I said, "No," as plain as day.

Lamont's funeral service was held at Campbell's on Madison Avenue. Aside from his family, almost everyone connected with the show attended. Jonathan Kramer was missing: "I had too much respect for Lamont to show up when it was well known that I didn't like him." Ronnie Dyson sang "You'll Never Walk Alone" without accompaniment. It wasn't what he sang so much as the way he sang it. He broke the whole place up. For most of us it was an agonizing experience.

I went to the burial. I don't remember who was or wasn't there; I only remember feeling bad. Afterwards some of the cast and I drove back to the theater with Robert I. Rubinsky.

It was somewhere between two and three in the afternoon and the audience was not quite full, sitting in the Biltmore theater waiting for *Hair* to begin. I guess some people couldn't wait. Michael Butler and the rest of management were standing outside the theater waiting for the cast to arrive. We were greeted by a flurry of waving management hands: "O.K. kids, hurry up. We're late. Hurry up, get inside. We'll park the car."

I got out to join Melba and her husband, George, who were sitting in another car waiting for Bob Chapman, a cast member. Some of the black kids had planned to meet back at the theater and then visit with Lamont's father to help console him, but we were so upset we decided against it. Donnie Burks, who was closest to Lamont, couldn't stop crying, nor could Emmeretta. I was cried out and felt torn apart inside.

The activity in front of the theater was frantic. We were being hassled to get inside. Someone in our car explained that we were not there to do the show, but to wait for Bob Chapman.

That's when the ranting and raving began. At this point I left the car to go to a pay phone. I was not about to go anywhere near the inside of the Biltmore, but I wanted to call the doorman, Russ, to relay a message from all the kids in our car: no matinee for us today.

Personally, I couldn't have done the matinee even if I wanted to. I felt emotionally and physically drained from the funeral and had a headache that was unreal.

On my way back to the car, Michael Butler stopped me. (I had successfully sidestepped his cronies.) He wanted to talk to me. Didn't we expect to do the show?

I explained how Ronnie and I and then the cast had gotten together with Fred Rheinglas to ask about closing this particular matinee. How most of them thought there should be no show that day. Michael Butler seemed genuinely surprised to hear all this. He acted as though he didn't know what was happening, or had happened. It's a possibility.

"I told Fred days before that this situation would probably arise," I said.

"We must stick together," Michael Butler said. "We are all members of the tribe. . . . Lamont would have wanted us to go on. . . . The show must go on."

I couldn't believe my ears. It was a complete about-face. Suddenly "Down with the theater Establishment" was changed to the biggest Broadway cliche of all time: "The show must go on."

A so-called tribal member was dead. The gesture of cancelling the matinee would have solidified the "tribe" and won Michael Butler universal respect, not to mention much sought-after free publicity. Was the house profit for one matinee worth it? I felt even sicker.

He then tried to talk me into getting the others to go on. If I wouldn't go on, would I get the others to do so, he asked. I told him flatly that I was not the leader; I wasn't leading anyone. The decision not to go on was not made as a group but individually. And I wouldn't ask anyone to do what I wasn't going to do.

"Lamont would have wanted you to do the show," he said.

I could no longer control myself. I read him then and there on the street in front of the whole world: all the things that were storing up in me since I had met him, all the anger over the bullshit that had been coming down since the beginning, which was now revealing itself for what it really was, came spilling out. The "love-rock tribal" bit just didn't work anymore. Least of all at that moment.

Michael Butler was turning all shades of green.

"We could fire you."

"I'm not going to kiss anybody's ass for no show!"

Back at the car, the other black kids were still being hassled to do the show. I told them what had happened and we all drove off to commiserate with one another.

The matinee show did go on, and I later heard from different people that it was a complete fiasco.

"It was an ugly situation," Jonathan Kramer said. "I sang 'Aquarius,' badly. Big Eddy of the band was tsk-tsking all the way through, that's how bad it was."

"While Jonathan was singing 'Aquarius,'" Robert I. told me, "Paul Jabara was saying, 'He's horrible. He has a vile voice.'"

"We were all looking at each other on that stage in disbelief," Paul Jabara said. "It was like a very sick dream."

"It's a strange thing," Jonathan said, "black people could play white roles, but white people couldn't play black roles. People read the black parts with scripts in their hands. Natalie Mosco played Abie. The part of Hud was split up all over the place. Jim Rado did some of it; I sang 'Colored Spade.' Whoever thought whites would have to do black parts?

"I had the words to 'White Boys' written on my hands. I spoke them. Imagine me singing in Melba's key? Paul Jabara was doing a dance up on that plank, and so was Robert I. The white girls were afraid to go up there, so we were the three drag queens in 'White Boys.'

"That night, the whites were so ashamed they were ready to take everything the blacks had to dish out. And they were dishing it out."

When the blacks returned to the theater, the tension was so thick you could cut it with a knife. Nobody had to say a word. It was all over for all of us. The kids who did the matinee kept coming up to me, trying to speak. "I have nothing to say," I told them. They sought me out in the dressing room. They had been "harassed," "threatened with being fired," and generally "intimidated" by management. "We had no choice!"

I finally told them that if they did what they thought was right, then why the excuses. Feeling as low as I did, I couldn't bear to listen to apologies and excuses. Almost all of them were talked onto the stage out of fear of losing their jobs. "You will never work again. We will take this to Equity," threatened management.

"We felt like field hands being coerced into something," Sally Eaton said.

Two people came right out with the truth. Hiram Keller told me that he would have been fired because he got in the show through a connection. Jonathan Kramer and Lamont, as everyone knew, didn't even speak to one another. Everyone else claimed that "no one was thinking in his (her) right mind."

"Melba changed dramatically," Jonathan Kramer said. "Up until that point we had been friends. That night she walked up to me and said, 'Shit. The reason you didn't go to Lamont's funeral wasn't because Lamont and you didn't like each other. You just wanted to be up on that platform singing "White Boys." ' That isn't true. But I let Melba yell at me. She was right to yell."

During the evening performance we all cried our way through the show. Everybody was crying—even some of the band and the stagehands. We were all emotional.

I felt sorry, too, for the white kids. That night was the first time I saw a black-power sign during "Let The Sun Shine In," our otherwise hand-holding finale. Eventually I used the sign myself. The black kids remained aloof throughout the performance, while the whites tried to integrate everything. They tried to make it seem as though it had never happened, and everything could go back to the way it was. Even in scenes when the cast is supposed to mix together, the stage was divided into black and white.

At the very top of the show, when Berger swings out over the audience singing "Donna," the cast sits behind him, usually haphazardly. That night blacks were on one side, whites on the other. It just happened.

From that point on, the feelings of the tribe—the trust, togetherness, comfort, contentment, even respect —were badly shaken. We still remained friendly toward each other and the management, but we were on our guard. The seed of suspicion had been planted and remained with most of us till we left the show. Of course we still enjoyed doing the show, but most of the genuine feeling was gone.

That day marked my first absence from the show. None of us were paid for the matinees on payday, however the following payday we were all mysteriously reimbursed. The money was in the checks and no one from management said anything about it.

The cast became more aware themselves after Lamont's death, and most of them realized a lot of what I projected was not hostility but awareness.

Some of the white kids said they had been approached by newsmen trying to find out what had happened. But they didn't want to talk about it. The incident was ugly enough among us and there was no need to spread it.

Management was afraid the black kids particularly would spill the entire story to the newspapers. They had reason to worry. As a group of us sat and talked at Donnie's house after the funeral the subject came up. We were all very angry. As we sat in various degrees of depression, someone said, "We should go to the papers."

Everyone (almost simultaneously): "I was thinking of that."

"We could go to the *Times*, the *Daily News*, all the papers."

"Don't forget the *Amsterdam News*."

"Yeah, we could really cook their goose."

"We could write up a statement and all sign it."

"Yeah, we should do it."

Then there were a few moments of silence as everyone thought.

"Maybe we shouldn't."

"Yeah."

"I don't want to hurt the show, I just want to pay them back for this whole incident."

"Yeah."

"Would the media listen to us?"

"I think we could cause them more discomfort by going back and not saying anything. Because they'll know we've got their number and we could go to the papers any time."

"Let's face it, what *Hair* has to say about freedom, love, and equality is valid, and it's reaching a lot of white people."

"Let's see what happens when we go back tonight. If they fire us we could still go."

Anyway the sweetest revenge of all was keeping management off balance. After we returned they didn't really know how to handle us or what we'd do next. They remained that way for months.

The situation between the cast was so shitty that Michael Butler called a tribal meeting in the back of the Biltmore. He and his cronies wanted to try to straighten things out. Nothing beats reality.

"If there's anything you're uptight about," they said, "you should bring it up at the meeting."

We did. The salary thing had been simmering all along. Before Lamont died the cast at least made it seem like a request. Now it was a demand: "We want more money." We didn't like the type of people they were bringing into the show. The cast wanted to sit in on auditions. Management made a lot of vague promises.

Toward the end of the meeting Robert I. piped up, "We haven't discussed the subject of the day of Lamont's funeral."

Michael Butler said, "I think it's tasteless to discuss that."

From that moment, the subject was closed to Michael Butler. He didn't want to discuss it. It was the first time I ever saw him so adamant about anything.

Management knew, as my brother Johnny put it, that "they blew it" and tried to make it up to us. We were bombarded with trust exercises and cast outings. Even another trip to Fire Island to try to reunify us.

We had one immediate problem. Donnie Burks, who was Lamont's understudy, temporarily took over the part of Hud, which meant that management needed an understudy for Hud. I was asked to try out, since I told Gerry and Galt I'd like to do the part.

Although I loved doing Abie, I was tired of playing the same thing and wanted to try something new. I also was all the more determined to get across the show's black message, such as it was, to the audience. Outside of pot and drugs, I believed in many of the things *Hair* had to say, especially as summed up by Hud, who has the line: "War is White people sending Black people to make war on Yellow people to defend the land they stole from Red people." Lamont was dead, but much of what he had given to the role of Hud still lived.

Hud is a very strong male role, so almost everyone was surprised when I took the part. I was a bit surprised myself, since I understood Michael Butler had to approve.

Professionally, playing Hud was a real challenge. One thing I felt I had gotten down was Hud's character. Aside from "Peter Professional," another cast nickname for Lamont was "Marvin Muscles." I decided to play Hud very butch, but to look very feminine. I wore hip-huggers, a halter top, and a headband.

The first night I went on as Hud I experienced my first case of bad stagefright since I started with *Hair*. I had only rehearsed the part a few times, and my one onstage dread is forgetting my lines. But as soon as I hit the stage and got into the role I began to pick up on the audience.

When I sang "Colored Spade" some people would slide into their seats; others would applaud; some would blank out by looking over at Claude, who is being tarred and feathered by three black girls, of whom I was usually one. The song never failed to get a reaction and I really dug doing the part.

The more I played Hud, some dozen times in all, the more uptight the cast seemed to become. Those in the cast who seemed to object most were those who seemed most concerned about their own status as male or female. Many of the gay girls were uptight; I could sense it. And some of the guys were jealous. I was good, I felt, and the audience applause told me that they dug me as Hud.

Then one day I was informed that a signed petition to give the understudy part of Hud to a guy, would be circulated at the next tribal meeting, which was to be held at the Good Doctor's office.

We all turned up at the Good Doctor's office one snowy night. The office furniture had been pushed to one side to give us room to sit on the floor. When the business of the petition came up, I explained that as an actress I saw nothing wrong with playing a male part. But most of the cast were unprofessional in their attitudes toward acting, and they found the idea too challenging to them on too many levels. Despite all the liberal talk of role-switching in *Hair*—there are "no black and white parts" and "all roles are interchangeable"—when it got down to the nitty-gritty, that, too, was bullshit. Although management didn't seem to mind, I finally agreed to give up understudying Hud. I didn't want to cause dissension among the cast. We had enough problems as it was.

32

One concession did emerge from our tribal meetings. Eventually *Hair* broke theater tradition and management finally gave the cast permission to sit in on auditions. I first sat in as a member of the cast, later as dance captain. While the cast had no control or power over who was hired, at least we naively thought our presence might have some influence on what type of person was hired.

Originally, Tom O'Horgan said, his "game" was for no one to know who he or she was playing in the show. Everyone would know the entire show, then pick a part out of a hat. "That's who you'd be."

Hair never stopped casting—for its road companies (three major ones named Jupiter, Venus, and Mercury), its out-of-town shows (Los Angeles, San Francisco, Chicago, Las Vegas, Boston, Seattle), its out-of-country productions (London, Toronto, Paris, Rome, Tokyo, Acapulco, Athens) and, above all, Broadway.

"*Hair*," said one company manager, referred to as the Dubious Wizard of the *Hair* office, "has never been taken out of the production situation."

Official auditions were conducted for the most part by Galt, Gerry, Jim, the casting agent of the moment, various assistant directors, Tom O'Horgan (when he was in town), and Michael Butler. Galt always struck me as someone who consistently knew what he was looking for.

Sitting in on auditions, I thought they seemed as much of an ordeal for the people casting as for those auditioning. Most of the people auditioning were embarrassing, some were merely awful. It was interesting to be on the other side of it for a change.

After *Hair* had become a Broadway sensation, I innocently assumed that aspiring theater people had some idea of what it was about. Or if not, that their own acts would at least keep pace with the times.

At one audition, a girl and a boy (they both looked like boys), identically dressed in tee shirts and jeans, sang something like "Tea for Two," accompanying themselves with a tap dance and a couple of acrobatic tricks.

Galt was laughing so hard he had to hide behind a *Life* magazine.

Gerry and Jim told me that during one audition an older woman sang some red-hot-momma type of song, clutching her overcoat the whole time. At the very end of her act, she flung open her coat to reveal that she was completely naked.

At another, a woman substituted dirty words for the lyrics to a song in the show; Gerry said it was hilarious.

The two best singers I heard in audition were hired by Galt, Gerry, and Jim—Sakinah Muhammad and Martha Valez. Martha sang through the entire audition chewing gum and still she was great.

Another very good audition was given by a blond boy of twenty-two or so who played guitar and sang like an angel. As it turned out, he had auditioned once before and was asked to come back, but went to jail instead for freaking out on drugs. I was dance captain at the time of his third audition, and Bob Currie, the production stage manager, Danny Sullivan, stage manager, and I all felt he was right for the show. He looked like a real flower child with his shoulder-length hair and beads, but from the way he talked he sounded like he had gone over once too often with drugs, even for *Hair*.

In November, 1969, *Hair* staged an open-call audition to fill in spots for their Toronto, Boston, and West Coast companies.

Tom O'Horgan, Danny Sullivan, Michael Butler, Gerry, and Jim were the primary judges.

During a break, a reporter covering the audition for the *Times** talked to Jim Rado. Jim was commenting

*Nov. 3, 1969, Howard Thompson

about an "intense" boy who had just tried out. "He is *Hair*—the freshness, right off the street, the way we first started.... When we first got here today and got out of the taxi, I heard one of the kids say, 'Here comes the professionals.' That really set me back."

And the way they were casting set the show back. It got worse and worse.

33

I suppose one reason *Hair* never stopped casting, particularly for the Broadway show, was because they never stopped firing people.

As early as Ukrainian Hall rehearsals, one of the stage managers noted in his book: "They are hiring and firing the wrong people."

Some people got fired who least expected it and others were kept on who should have been dropped. It happened over and over again. I stopped counting the *Hair Playbills* at sixteen.

One ex-publicity agent for *Hair* said that one day they were all talking about astrology at a production meeting and he made the mistake of confessing that he was a Libra. Supposedly, someone high in management, a Sagittarian, bowed his head solemnly and the next day the guy was fired.

Considering the hiring and firing practices of the show, it's not too hard to believe.

I even got involved myself. At one point there was a rumor going around that I was responsible for people getting fired. People were being fired left and right. My nickname Hannah Hostile had been changed to Mary Mouth.

One evening after a performance, Michael Butler invited the cast to a late dinner at Jim Downey's. This was one of the rare instances of a tribal meeting with the chief, alone.

After we finished, those in the cast who were so inclined were invited to go up to his table, one by one, to talk over whatever problems they had.

When my turn came I told him about the rumor circulating about my firing powers. I said I wasn't sure who started it.

Michael Butler said that if the cast was dumb enough to think I had the power to get people fired, then let them believe it.

As long as he knew about it I no longer cared. It was never brought up again. The rumor eventually fizzled out, although I finally traced it to its source: Elsie Dyson.

Elsie was becoming a real problem backstage, and it got increasingly worse as the show wore on. Ronnie was rarely free to do anything, even go to dinner after the show, without his mother tagging along.

There was a Mr. Dyson, but he was so quiet that you hardly ever knew he was present.

One day backstage, Ronnie said to Elsie, "Mommy, I wish you wouldn't come to the theater, because you make me nervous when you're in the audience."

She looked at him as if he'd slapped her across the face. Then she lit into him, "Don't you talk to me like that, telling me about how nervous I make you. . . ."

"It's time," I often thought, "for Elsie to be written out of the act."

I tried to tell Elsie any number of times what she was doing to Ronnie. She never listened, never wanted to know. Sometimes she became loud and angry. We are good friends still, mainly because I listen to her, and neither one of us takes shit from anyone, including each other.

Like so many others, Ronnie quit the show at one point, then came back. On the day of his return, Julie Arenal and I were standing backstage, talking. Suddenly, Julie, who was facing the stage door, got a strange expression on her face.

Elsie was standing right behind me. She said to me, "Now that Ronnie is coming back to the show, you're going to have to give him back his part, because he's the star of this show!"

"I'm only doing *one* of his lines," I said.

"Well, you're going to have to give it back to him, honey."

I don't like being attacked for no apparent reason. Although I was angry, I was brought up to respect adults no matter what.

As calmly as possible, I said, "Elsie, I'm going to walk away. If you don't want trouble, you'll stay away from me."

Walking upstairs I was on the verge of tears, I was so frustrated; I felt a tugging at my sweater.

It was Elsie. "You know I was only kidding," she said.

While I was trying to reach the next step, she kept tugging at my sweater, crying and trying to reason with me at the same time. She apologized to the point where I gave in.

One evening after a show, Ronnie, Elsie, and I were standing on a street corner when an older woman, who was drunk and looked like a hooker, walked by and brushed up against Ronnie. It could have been accidental, but Elsie saw it too. She read the poor woman then and there.

The woman was startled for a moment, then pulled herself together. "Miss," she said to Elsie, "I don't want your son."

I was laughing so hard I missed the rest. If you didn't laugh at Elsie, you wanted to weep.

The cast reacted much the same way to the constant firings. After a while it became one big cast joke.

It was bad enough that no-talents were being hired, even for lead parts; often those who had been hired were fired, then rehired only to be fired again a few months later.

One girl was fired and rehired within an hour because she cried and begged to be taken back. Then she got an attitude when she discovered she wasn't being given back the part she had originally been fired from.

Jonathan Kramer was fired "once every three hundred performances," and Emmeretta Marks was fired and rehired three times (by my count). So was Linda Compton.

Steve Gamet left the show and then was rehired to do Claude. Soon afterwards he left the show for good.

It also wasn't unusual for people to be fired from one company and hired for another. This was true of staff as well as cast. Stage managers were often fired from one company, only to show up in another in a higher position within the *Hair* organization. It also happened in reverse.

Sometimes people would be fired and you wouldn't learn it until days later. Other times a cast member would be out sick and no one knew whether he was fired or not.

Very few of the cast simply quit the show. About six or seven months after we opened, the topic of Steve Curry again dominated one of our tribal meetings. This was another of those exceptional times when we met with the chief alone. He came without any of his cronies. Steve had been fired for the third and last time. Michael Butler came to tell us he'd had nothing to do with it.

Gerry and Jim, who were doing *Hair* in Los Angeles, flew in to deny that they had had anything to do with it either. It was pass-the-buck time.

The assistant director, Glen Nielson, was the one who told Steve he was fired. But who authorized Glen to do the firing? The Phantom?

Glen Nielson and Steve Curry never got along. Glen was a script-stickler. He was always trying to get the cast to take it as literally as possible. "You have to stick to the script," he would say. Steve Curry used to whistle when Glen was trying to get Steve to follow a script line word for word.

During rehearsal one day, Glen and Steve had a more heated argument than usual. Glen wanted Steve, as Berger, to say one line exactly as written in the script, but the very next performance Steve changed one word of the line. That, ostensibly, is why Steve was fired.

Of all the cast, the two Steves (Curry and Gamet)

could get away with virtually anything. During one matinee performance, shortly after they wrecked their dressing room, they threw the mud from the tar and feather scene at the first three rows of the audience. The audience wasn't too pleased. Both Steves were reprimanded by the acting stage manager and the matter was dropped. Changing one word seemed mighty trivial in comparison.

So everyone in the cast was shocked when Steve Curry was finally fired. We thought he was an integral part of the show, and letting him go broke our spirit. A solo appearance by our chief at a tribal meeting meant it was serious. Michael Butler was still trying to hold the cast together.

During Steve's last performance we all cried onstage; afterwards we held a party for him backstage.

34

Whenever a member of the cast, particularly someone we liked, left the show, we held a brief farewell party backstage during intermission. Everyone in the production was invited. Generally wine or champagne, sometimes a cake, was provided.

Besides the intermission send-offs, the cast would also plan a little "surprise" onstage for whoever was leaving that night. Last performances were always more vibrant, especially for members of the original cast.

I planned a little "surprise" for Donnie Burks' last performance. We had a scene together in which he plays Hud as a black militant to my Abe. He has a few hate-filled lines in which he says he's going to cut me up. I'm lying down, supposedly shot from the previous scene.

On Donnie's last night, after he finished his lines, I stood up and, instead of saying my lines, gave him a long kiss. If you changed anything on Donnie, he would die of embarrassment, so I knew the kiss would shake him up.

Woof, usually played by a white boy, was played by Ronnie Dyson for his last performance. But instead of surprising him with a poster of Mick Jagger, we handed him a poster of George Wallace. To say his surprise was genuine is putting it mildly. But that was less embarrassing than the night Erik Robinson left the show. Someone put a whoopee-cushion (which makes a fartlike noise) on his chair during one of the quieter scenes in the show.

Sometimes such incidents were accidental. One night when Melba Moore stood up for the roll call scene, the audience roared with laughter. One of her breasts was sticking out of her shirt. She looked down, tucked it back into her shirt and said her lines.

During the war scene after one send-off party, Allan Nicholls pushed me so hard I fell off the stage, backwards. Luckily the musicians' truck broke my fall, but still I was out for a week with contusions. I got paid for the time out, but I was pissed off. It always made more sense to me to hold the send-off parties after the show. *Hair* was difficult enough to do straight.

The stage manager wanted me to tell Equity that I had fallen off the stage rather than been pushed. I guess he was trying to protect himself. He was at the send-off party, too, and any acting up during a performance would be his responsibility.

I got a taste of that kind of responsibility myself after Diane Keaton left the show to do "Play It Again, Sam." The cast elected me to replace her as chorus Equity deputy. Sally Eaton replaced Lamont as Equity deputy for the principals.

The job, as it turned out, is a bitch. An Equity deputy acts as an intermediary between management and the cast. No one but a theatrical lawyer could know enough to answer all the questions. Most of the cast expected me to know all the legalities concerning work hours, picture calls, contracts, wages, vacation time, and so on. Or even worse, they expected me to get involved with their personal problems with management. Hearing people constantly gripe and whine was a drag, especially when any attempt to try to do something was generally unappreciated. At times like these the "love tribe" went on the warpath—and the squaw with the squawks was me.

CAST MEMBER: I got docked in my pay for being late last week.
ME: Were you late?
CAST MEMBER: Well, yes . . . .
ME: What can I do about it?

Most of the cast saw the job as some kind of promotion within the *Hair* company. It was a status symbol, something to boost their egos. I gave up the job to George Tipton after about five minths.

Whenever I had problems at the theater, I didn't mess around with the Equity deputy; I went straight to

Equity. Even if they didn't have the answers, they would try to find them for you.

Knowing a few answers would have helped all of us, particularly Paul Jabara the night he was fired in the midst of a performance.

"They fired me as a matter of discipline," he told me.

"I believe I was doing a good job, and they knew I was doing a good job. For no apparent reason they were playing with my head.

"The night I was fired, a big producer, Hilly Elkins [*O! Calcutta!, The Rothschilds, Alice's Restaurant*] had come to see me in the show. I was playing the part of Woof, but preferred to play Mom, my original part, because I was good in my part. It was *my* part.

"They didn't want me to do Mom that night. I said, 'Look. I'd rather do my part, one which I have been reviewed for, rather than someone else's part.' Apparently, management felt I was doing too much in the show that night. I was playing Woof, Margaret Mead, and Electric Blues, and that, they felt, was enough.

" 'Then I don't want to go on,' I told them. 'You've called me when ten people were out sick, supposedly, and I always came in, even if I was sick myself.' Fred Rheinglas would call me up and say, 'Paul, please come in. We don't have anybody.' I would come in and do a million different roles, a million different parts.

"So I gave them an ultimatum: either I do what I want to do, or I'm not going to go on. I was being a prima donna, but I felt I was right. I'd worked my ass off for that show. They still said no.

"I went to the back of the house as soon as the music started. When the show began, I couldn't resist: I had to go on. I ran backstage, put on my Woof costume, and started to go onstage.

"'Where do you think you're going?' they said.

"'Onstage.'

"'No you're not. You said you weren't going on. Go home. No one is indispensible.'

"I told them I *had* to go on. They kept saying, 'Go home. We'll see you tomorrow.'

"At that point I darted past them and went onstage.

"It was so ridiculous, because what it had become was a sudden matter of discipline. It was management against actors. They tried to pull me offstage. I wasn't doing anything, just playing my part, but they had three people trying to pull me off. There was even a cop saying, 'Should I get him? Should I get him?'

"Everyone was saying, 'Paul, go off.' But everyone knew that if they approached me to try to get me off that stage I would cause such a scene that they wouldn't know what to do.

"Finally, when the Mom scene came up, I put my costume on and they said, 'Get that costume off.'

"'This is my costume.'

"'Get it off.'

"We went on like that until you [me] turned to me, you were just as freaked out as everybody else, and you said, 'Paul, give me the costume.'"

I was the understudy for Mom that night. Paul would have been better off doing Mom, but they just wouldn't let him. It was a real hassle. I saw basically what was happening, and it just wasn't worth it. They were after him, but he wouldn't quit. There was a lot of out-shouting. Finally, Fred turned to Paul and said, "You're finished, baby!"

"What movie did you get that line from?" Paul said.

"You'll never work again in this theater."

"With pleasure," Paul said, throwing the costume away and walking out.

I picked it up, put it on, and went on. Paul was fired.

"I watched the rest of the show," he said. "I was so freaked out. It was management against actors. I said to some of the kids, 'Don't you understand? If we're going to stick together, let's stick together now. They've been screwing us so much. We are the show!'

"The kids didn't care. They only cared when it was something happening to them. But it referred to me at the moment, and no one stuck behind me at all."

35

All of us in the original Broadway cast knew we were unique, the first of a kind, because everyone said so— friends, fans, staff, the media. But the more *Hair* companies that opened around the country, then the world— other shows such as *My Fair Lady* may have been more widely distributed, but *Hair* has "traveled farther faster than any other show in history"*—the more it seemed as if all the stories about *Hair* mismanagement and the love bullshit were the same; only the names and places were different.

**Hair*: That Play Is Sprouting Everywhere, *Life* Magazine, Tom Prideaux

As *Hair* grew, it fell apart. Everybody had the same stories; it seemed as if the flaws were built into the nature of the show and were bound to turn up from one company to the next. With *Hair* scattered to the four winds, the producer—our "chief"—couldn't keep track of everything or everyone, a girl in the New York *Hair* office told me. He wasn't informed of all that went on; he didn't interview people anymore. People could cover up their mistakes without being detected for a long time. "Everyone wanted to look good in Michael Butler's eyes," she said.

Hair opened in Los Angeles on November 22, 1968. Soon after, kids from the L.A. show began to appear in the Broadway *Hair,* and vice-versa. Much of what they told us paralleled the New York scene.

The L.A. opening was very similar to New York's, only it was *Hair* à la Hollywood. The specially invited first night audience was "stuffy" at first, but wound up digging the show. Gerry and Jim, on a leave of absence from the New York company, starred as Berger and Claude. For the première the "chief of the tribe," Michael Butler, was painted silver to play the part of a silver Indian. Afterwards, John and Michelle Phillips, two of The Mommas and Poppas, threw a party for the cast in their Beverly Hills home.

Before the opening Tom O'Horgan had gone out to Los Angeles to do his "skin language" number on the cast. Tom's "magic" seemed to work just as well with the L.A. "tribe" in the beginning as it had with New York's.

"There was the same 'love' thing," one girl from the L.A. cast said. "It was real."

"I thought the Los Angeles company was much more family-oriented towards one another," said Erik Robinson, "like it was in the New York company when we first went out to Fire Island."

For all the parallels, one major difference seemed to be drugs and sex. Apparently neither was as rampant in the Los Angeles company, or at least not as up-front. One girl told me that Narks hung around the theater a lot, and both she and another guy said there weren't many orgies backstage. At least nobody tripped over people screwing in the dressing rooms.

But outside the dressing rooms it was another story. Six or seven weeks after Erik Robinson joined the L.A. production of *Hair,* he was invited to Jim Rado's birthday party.

He was told to come to the party totally nude except for a paper bag over his head with two eyeholes cut out. Since everyone from the *Hair* cast had done the nude scene, the idea was to recognize bodies instead of faces. Erik said he had never participated in the New York dressing-room gang bangs, so before entering the party, he had second thoughts. He peeked in the window from the porch: everybody was fully clothed.

Erik put his clothes back on, and went inside. The place was jammed. It was a big house and the main party decor was toilet-paper streamers. They were everywhere. Each room in the house seemed to have its own thing going. One was for smoking, another for dancing to live music, and still another to taped music. Of about a hundred people, approximately twenty-five were from *Hair.*

Erik bumped into a girl he'd gone to school with. "We had always been attracted to one another, but never got around to doing anything about it.

"To make up for lost time," Erik said, "we started

making out in the hall. One thing lead to another, and the next thing we knew, we were on the floor under a table in the hallway. We started removing our clothes. People complained: 'Do that up in the bedroom where it belongs.'

"We made our way, and each other, up the steps and finally to a bedroom. En route, we discarded more clothes so that by the time we got there we were totally naked. We were really going now, making love in various ways and positions, completely into each other and oblivious to anyone else.

"Suddenly, it was like Paramount presents: people started filling up the room, taking seats to watch. Some were getting off on it themselves. They were into a voyeur's thing. Others were making rude comments. Some clucked, 'Shame, shame,' and others said, 'Fuck her, boy!'

"Our little twosome soon developed into a fivesome, two girls and three guys. A couple of people were standing around naked, watching, but not participating. Other groups formed but didn't take off all their clothes."

The whole scene turned into a sex-travaganza which lasted about four hours with a constantly changing audience.

"One of the original girls left the group when the other girl made a pass at her. The two original stars, myself and the girl, lasted longer than anyone, with the exception of one other fellow who was amazing.

"Another guy, who had stripped down completely and was taking part, spoke a few incantations over us, trying to seduce other people into the act. He sort of meditated over the group naked.

"Still another guy immediately assumed the position of director. He began calling out directions for different scenes and different combinations. It sounded very much like the lyrics from 'Sodomy,' one of the songs in *Hair*."

Apparently the orgy got heavier and heavier. "We even did a shower scene."

Right in the middle of the whole scene, the girl Erik was going with at the time, someone on the *Hair* staff, walked in. "She was very supercool about it. She never said a word to me."

Some time later, Erik and a bunch of the cast went to the San Francisco opening of *Hair*. I had heard that when Tom O'Horgan auditioned for the San Francisco show, he didn't want any kids who had been in previous *Hair* companies. It was like he really wanted to start fresh.

After the opening, Gerry, Jim, Erik, Oatis Stephens, and Heather MacRae drove up to San Francisco. They were all standing in the back of the Aquarius Theater when Gerry said to them, "Let's give this thing a boost."

According to Erik the show by then was "in poor shape in terms of energy, excitement, and getting a good rapport with the audience. Compared to what it had been, it was pretty low."

Gerry's idea of a "boost" was for all the guys to strip and when the "cops" came out at the end of Act I they'd walk down the center aisle nude.

Heather held their clothes and waited for them in the back. "She couldn't believe we were going to do it," Erik said. "She thought it was all a big joke."

When several people in the audience saw the four naked guys, they yelled, "Far out!," "Great!," and "Keep it up!"

Encouraged, they all went up onstage, turned around to face the audience, and waved. Then they walked off to cheers. The cast cop just stood there scratching his head.

The next day Erik received a communication through the P.R. man from Michael Butler stating that Erik would not be allowed in any of the *Hair* theaters unless he wrote a letter of apology saying that he was sorry for causing a certain amount of trouble.

"I thought that was amusing since it did provide a certain amount of free publicity for the show," Erik said. He never wrote the letter of apology.

The Los Angeles tribal meetings, or gripe sessions, were "just one part of the parties Michael Butler threw," said a guy from the original L.A. cast.

"Someone would run around announcing that a big gripe session was going to be held at Michael Butler's house in the Hollywood Hills. Usually I'd skip them, curry dinners and all, because they were upsetting. Instead of getting down to real issues, we'd get down to petty shit, personal ego-trip shit.

"The first gripe session turned into cut-throat warfare. One girl [who eventually joined the New York show] left the room crying. Favorites were obviously played by management."

"I think more harm was done than not," a girl from the L.A. cast said.

"One month after *Hair* opened in L.A.," the guy from the original L.A. cast continued, "Dick Osorio, the company manager, told us: 'There are two *Hairs*. One onstage, and one in the front office that's making money. Don't compare the two. They support each other and that's about it. We are in this to make money and we don't subscribe to the *Hair* philosophy in the front office.'

"We were working with Tom and we couldn't see it," the same guy said. "We couldn't see the contradictions yet."

But as soon as the money started rolling in, the contradictions became obvious. Of course the same thing happens in all shows, but in *Hair* they kept telling us it wasn't happening. They were still cramming *Love* down our throats.

A man on the street once asked me what *Hair* was about. I said, "Mister, look at the left-hand corner of your ticket stub, where the price of the ticket is printed. That's what it's about."

Barry McGuire finally left the New York show when he saw what was happening with management. He really got disillusioned. Barry went out to California as a member of the L.A. production staff. Supposedly, he didn't even stay long enough to sign a contract.

Absenteeism was also a big hassle with the Los Angeles company. "We averaged fifty some odd absences a week," the guy from L.A. said. "They passed a rule that we couldn't stay out without a doctor's note, but it didn't work." Mainly because the ones who least deserved it got hit the hardest by the rule. This particular cast member, one of the workhorses, got fired because he was late due to car trouble and had no doctor's excuse.

While he was in the New York show he said, "You'd be surprised how alike people are from cast to cast—the workhorses, the gig-doers, the superstars, the ones who are allowed to stay on—and you wonder why, or how, they got into the show in the first place."

"When the original company split up and new people came in, the show began to deteriorate," one girl from the L.A. cast said.

According to the guy from the original L.A. cast, Gerry and Jim caused a sensation while they were there.

"Gerry is a man of the moment. Berger is fashioned after someone in real life. Gerry became Berger.

"I have a lot of respect for Gerry's genius," he went on, "but I find him very violent and thoughtless. Gerry hurt me physically on a number of occasions when I was working with him onstage."

Gerry and Jim had a way of keeping the Los Angeles as well as the New York cast in a constant state of turmoil. Besides pitting people against each other, usually cast and management, they were always making promises, usually echoes of Tom O'Horgan's ideas: we're all going to live together; we'll have an actors' workshop; we won't charge admission; we won't have anything to do with management.

"Michael Butler didn't like them around," the guy from L.A. said. "Every time Gerry and Jim came into the show there was trouble. They created chaos.

"Gerry used to bring guys, people he knew, right up onstage and into the actual show. The cast used to get really upset about that. From what I understood Paul Jabara had a lot to do with the shaping of *Hair*. When he left the New York show he was in a bad way, and Gerry wanted him to do a few parts in our show on opening night. The cast said, 'absolutely not!'

"On opening night I was doing a line, when Paul came out of the audience saying, 'Wait a minute, wait a minute,' and did the line.

"The cast looked at one another. 'What's going on?' "

It was everybody's favorite question concerning the two heads of *Hair*, including Tom O'Horgan.

"Every time I go there [L.A.] I freak out because

of some incident," he said. "If you think it's bad in New York, you couldn't believe L.A. At the end of the show one time, they had a whole line of thug-ushers standing there like S.S. troops, arm in arm, across the front of the stage while people were singing and dancing. Because of some fire law or something only a hundred people were allowed onstage. But what were they trying to do?

"And every time I'd go into the theater, I'd get hassled in some way. I didn't go very often, and the help changes constantly, but one night the bartender didn't know who I was. He just had a really rough, nasty kind of tactic. 'I'm the director of the show,' I said.

" 'Yeah, so am I,' he said.

"I'd get so furious. I could have had him fired, but then I said to myself: What are you doing? You're doing the same thing he is. I had to prove who I was. I don't care about that. What bothered me was the fact that if I was being treated that way, how were they treating the customers?

"The kids onstage are breaking their asses to prove that there is such a thing as love left in the world, and here, at the theater, everyone is being treated like a used-car lot.

"And they wonder why Gerry goes there and freaks out. Every time he goes there he sees something monstrous going on and completely goes crazy. He's done some insane things—like running through the audience naked. Management wonders why."

36

After a while, nobody in New York knew who was running
the show. Gerry and Jim ran it one week, Michael Butler
the next, Tom O'Horgan the week after that. There was
a kind of tribal leader of tug-of-war going on, especially
between Gerry and Jim and Michael Butler.

Hair was simply going to their heads. For instance,
Michael Butler once held a big powwow in Oak Brook,
Illinois. None of the cast was invited, or any one who
had helped create *Hair,* just bookkeepers, accountants,
and coordinators.

"Everybody slept around the 'chief's' house in their
tents," said a girl from the New York *Hair* office. "He
was building a little empire for himself. I had to call
him at one point. Not sure who had picked up on the
other line, I asked, 'Is this Michael Butler?'

" 'Yes,' he said, 'this is your great white father speaking.' "

The girl said she had left *Hair* for a while and when
she returned, the attitude of the New York office toward
the actors was that "actors are like third-class people.

When there was just the New York company, this wasn't so. As far as management was concerned, it became an ego-thing."

One end was pulling against the other. The power feud peaked when Gerry and Jim returned from doing their thing in Los Angeles. *Hair*'s private wars finally became public pulp. What happened spilled over into the newspapers.

After their return from L.A., Gerry and Jim began cutting up onstage even more than usual. Something different was happening every performance. Though they later claimed they were following improvisations they had used with management's approval in L.A., as far as I knew they never told anyone what they were going to do; they just did it. There was an increase in what the papers called "salacious" acts: there was more "hump" in the "humping" onstage during and after the simulated tease-sex scenes. There was also more free-form nudity.

One night while Jim, fully clothed, was singing "Where Do I Go?" and all the other *sedentary* nudes were already standing in place, Gerry and Sally Eaton walked nude from the wings to the platform. Another time, there was an added nude attraction when a guy wearing nothing more than Day-Glo paint turned up during the "Electric Blues" number.

Getting the straight story of the behind-the-scenes happenings at *Hair* was difficult enough under ordinary circumstances, but with the tribe in full rebellion, and with the air thick with claims and counterclaims from both sides, even the press couldn't keep it all straight.

Gerry and Jim maintained they were willing to scratch anything management found "objectionable" in the performances, but just exactly what was objectionable was never made clear in the newspaper reports. *Variety* reported that they "indulged in prolonged nudity and *graphic* miming of a variety of sex acts onstage."*

Fearing a possible police bust, Michael Butler reportedly told Gerry and Jim not to go on one night, but when they turned up to watch the show with the regular audience, a man in the lobby told them they couldn't even enter the theater.

The next day, at the four-o'clock rehearsal, they appeared at the theater to wait for their lawyer, who, when he arrived, told them that though they had been dismissed from the cast and had been paid off under their contracts as actors, they were still entitled to watch the rehearsals as authors. But Victor Samrock,*Hair*'s general manager, informed them he had instructions not to allow either one to enter the theater, in any capacity.

Gerry and Jim were upset, but on their lawyer's advice they left without much trouble. "They asked us to come back from Los Angeles to take up our parts. . . ." Jim said outside. Then, waving at an armored truck that had come to pick up receipts from the box-office, he said, "I wish it would close, it doesn't belong here. . . . The management turns out to be our enemy. . . . That's the very thing we're writing about."**

Some time after this episode, I tape-recorded Jim saying, "We're all emotional at *Hair,* because we're waging the very war we wrote about, at the theater with management."

Management had been after their ass and suddenly, instant enlightenment. "We're in an isolation ward," Jim

*April 16, 1969
**N.Y. *Times,* April 12, 1969

said. "Before we leave we really want to make it what it should have been and never was." (He also admitted to me that leaving the New York show to go to L.A. had been their biggest mistake in the first place.)

Both sides shot arrows at each other for several days. Now that they were finally barred from the Biltmore, Gerry and Jim threatened to cancel Michael Butler's rights to the show. They claimed Michael Butler had asked them to do the new L.A. bits onstage. Management denied that. Gerry and Jim's contracts were terminated for "deviating from the standard performance in violation of the Equity production contract."*

Gerry and Jim pressed charges with the Dramatists Guild alleging that Michael Butler had violated the authors' rights to attend all rehearsals and performances. Moreover, Michael Butler was in violation of contract by hiring people without Gerry and Jim's approval. To top it off, Gerry and Jim said that Michael Butler made changes in the script without their okay.

I couldn't understand what all the fuss was about; hardly a night went by when somebody wasn't making some kind of change in the "script."

The authors of *Hair,* Gerry, Jim, and Galt, had been receiving weekly payments of 7½ percent of the gross, out of which 1½ percent went to the New York Shakespeare Festival. According to *Variety,*** *Hair* "has been grossing a capacity of $66,000-plus since its opening, so the three authors have been splitting slightly less than $4,000 a week."

Finally the "chief of the tribe" offered to smoke the peace-pipe with his two delinquent "braves" and invited Gerry, Jim, and Galt to meet with him at the home of

*Variety, April 16, 1969
**Variety, April 16, 1969

a friend and business associate, Peter Yarrow (formerly of Peter, Paul, and Mary). They suggested meeting at the Sheep Meadow in Central Park, near the zoo, instead. After a long powwow, all charges were dropped. Truce had been declared.

Supposedly, what burned Michael Butler even more than the "objectionable" material was that he was not being notified about the changes in the show. But he soon gave approval, and much of the L.A. improv was eventually incorporated into the Broadway performance.

Nearly a week later it was reported in *Variety** that the whole thing had been touched off when the owner of the Biltmore Theater warned Michael Butler that if Gerry and Jim were busted and the show had to be closed as a result, he would bring *Hair* up on charges. The cast understood that Biltmore management had agreed to one nude scene—as long as all the nudes stood perfectly still. Under New York law at the time, nudity was permitted unless the "nude becomes lewd."

Variety said, "At the Central Park conference, the producer and the authors agreed to stand together in the event of police intervention."

After the feud, Gerry and Jim were told that they were free to attend all rehearsals and performances and to approve all cast replacements.

Ben Vereen, the first black Broadway Berger, and Richard Kim Milford, who filled in as Claude, dropped back to understudies for Gerry and Jim. Shortly after that Ben Vereen was fired. The complaint was that he was "too Broadway," but many thought he was almost as good as Gerry.

Henceforth, the item in *Variety* noted, any tribal dif-

*April 23, 1969

ficulties between the Big Chief and his two top Braves over the script would be settled by a consultation with a third member of the *Hair* tribal council, Tom O'Horgan.

Gerry and Jim returned to the show just in time for the 1969 Tony awards presentation. *Hair* had been chosen to perform for the TV broadcast, and also nominated for three categories: Best Musical, Best Director, and Best Musical Score.

37

We all knew we deserved to win a Tony award, especially as Best Musical, but we all knew we wouldn't. *Hair* was the first of its kind; it was the most creative piece of work on Broadway that year. To some, we were a raggle-taggle of long-haired, dirty hippie weirdos just "doing our thing" onstage, but we all knew the revolution we had set off in theater, fashion, drug culture, hippie lifestyle. Perhaps it was just as well that we had missed being eligible for 1968's Tony award nominations, because even one year later, nudity, freedom, and just plain fun onstage still was not accepted over the polished, formula theatrics to which the Broadway Establishment was accustomed. It was primarily for that reason that Tom O'Horgan said he could "afford to be more outrageous uptown than downtown."

The attitude of the Tony awards was similar to that

of our opening night audience: no one was too sure how to react.

We were scheduled to perform along with such Establishment musicals as *1776* and *Promises, Promises*. I sat in the audience of the Mark Hellinger theater and watched *Promises, Promises* go through its rehearsals like clockwork. I had seen a preview of the show, and now I decided it was in no way better than *Hair*. Different, but not better.

Throughout the day we talked to a lot of celebrities—Pearl Bailey, Harry Belafonte. He kissed my hand. *Is he kidding?* He's even more handsome in person than on the screen. I was really feeling good until Julie Arenal called us for a warm-up rehearsal of the dances.

Downstairs, in a sort of lounge-cafeteria, approximately twenty-four of us began writhing on the floor, going through our thing. It was old hat to us, but apparently weird to the other performers who watched us with strange expressions on their faces.

At one point Shelley Winters joined us. She got down on the floor and started miming our movements. She was just horsing around, but the stage manager asked her to leave, explaining that we were "rehearsing." Most of the cast admitted they felt stupid. For the first time outsiders were getting an inside look at *Hair*. It was like spilling open a bag of dirty laundry. We were so self-conscious that we rushed to get through the exercises.

The next step down was when we finally moved the rehearsal onstage. Performers from the other shows sat and watched us, just as we had them. For some reason we couldn't get the music together. The band was placed on one level and we were on another. Gerri Griffin and Sakinah, who were going to sing "What A Piece of Work

Is Man," couldn't get the harmony straight. When Galt, who was conducting, asked Melba to replace Gerri, most of the cast felt the blame was being put on the wrong person; we wasted almost a half hour haggling over it.

To us such hassles were routine, but letting it all hang out for an audience was embarrassing. Who waits until the last minute to decide who's going to do what on coast-to-coast television?

Things were so far down they just got worse. By the time we'd finished rehearsing, our *Hair* dresser came onstage and dumped our costumes in a heap. Steve Gamet and I were among the last to rummage through them, looking for ours. One of the Tony show's assistants told us to "get the hell off the stage." Just as I was picking up my stuff he yelled again.

When I asked him to give us a second, he threatened to bar me from doing the show. Then he stormed over to Alexander Cohen, who was nearby, and started bad-mouthing me. Much to the assistant's surprise, I marched over to Mr. Cohen to defend myself. The producer calmly put his arm around me and walked me away from the scene, saying not to pay the guy any mind, "We're all tense."

If any one thing summed up the difference between *Hair* and the Establishment it was the scene in the girls' dressing room. The costumes for the cast of *Promises, Promises* were all hung neatly on hangers; their shoes, high-heeled, were neatly lined up on the dressing table in an array of beautiful colors. Our costumes were dumped to the side, and scattered in a pile were our worn shoes.

I loved every minute of standing in the wings, rubbing shoulders with the stars, waiting to go on. From the stage

I saw Michael Butler sitting in the audience in full dress. "That's where he belongs," I thought. Like most of the audience, he appeared stiff and formal; although there were variations in dress, everyone looked alike. I felt sorry for Michael Butler, because he, too, was going to be cheated of the victory.

Our cue. The anger that we all felt had keyed us up—we gave a very strong performance.

When the winner for the Best Musical was announced, I was surprised. Not that we didn't win, but that *1776* did. I was suddenly struck by the irony: here was a musical about America's revolutionary past pitted against one about America's revolutionary present. Broadway in 1969 still wasn't ready for *Hair*.

We also lost in the categories of Best Director and Best Musical Score. There was a lot of groaning and crying backstage, some of it from other performers. The whole experience left most of the cast feeling empty. Even people around the stage door commiserated with us. "You should have won," we heard over and over again. It was like a chant, and it was beginning to get on my nerves.

A formally dressed couple getting into a chauffer-driven limousine yelled out of their window: "You kids were marvelous. You should have won!"

"If we were so great, why didn't you vote for us?," I yelled back.

They slumped far back in their seats and the chauffer drove them away.

The band was the real tipoff. When they went sour we had problems.

Of all the reactions to our performance, I valued the band's most. Except for a short time when management tried to block them from the audience's view with a screen (to avoid having to pay them extra for being onstage), they saw the show night after night. "Every night, every show, you know something is going to happen," Eddy Williams said. He thought the constant changes were good. In fact, Jonathan Kramer thought Eddy was *the* critic of the show; "If he didn't like the way you sang, he played flat notes during your song. If he didn't like the way you were acting, he talked during your monologue."

"I knew that if I finished a certain line completely," Paul Jabara said, "and the music came in at the right time, I could do a particular take and get a laugh. If the band missed the beat, it would be off and wouldn't work. It was all timing and instinct. I used to try to get them to do it. Sometimes they would and sometimes they wouldn't."

If the band liked your performance, they didn't hesitate to tell you. You could also hear them laughing and applauding from behind. Sometimes their carrying-on was picked up by the live mikes and could be heard throughout the audience, who probably thought it was part of the anything-goes atmosphere.

And sometimes, as one critic, Stewart Klein of WNEW-TV put it, ". . . the screaming decibel-level of the show" might "give you a headache."

More often than not, that's exactly what it did do to the sound department. One of the sound men noted in his log: "Band level is the highest it's ever been, with everybody in competition with each other. I cannot get the voices over the band and keep them sounding good or even O.K. I have to drive the singers to distortion to be heard."

I never felt driven to "distortion" in *Hair*, only distraction.

I didn't even have to look over at the bandstand to know when Jimmy or Idris (the rhythm section) were out; I could hear it from the difference in sound. They were fabulous. The sound man found control easier because "a substitute does not play as loud as the regular man."

The band goofed only once during my entire run with the show. It was the time when Clive Barnes of the New York *Times* came to reappraise *Hair*.

A week before his anticipated appearance, management descended upon the cast in full force. Gerry and Jim, still with the L.A. troupe, flew in from the Coast just to do one performance. To justify giving them back their original parts, Michael Butler told us how much it would mean to us to get a good review.

The entire cast said no. It was unanimous. Barry McGuire and Joe Butler would go on as they always did. Gerry and Jim couldn't force the decision, because they realized it would hurt the show even more, so they didn't go on. We were in bad shape. *Hair* was nowhere near as good as the first time Clive Barnes had seen it on Broadway about nine months earlier.

Tom and Galt returned for the occasion to put us through marathon rehearsals once again, only this time they degenerated into chaos. There were endless petty arguments. The show seemed worse than it had during our pre-opening night rehearsal period.

The bad vibes spoiled the overall performance. Even if the audience didn't pick up on our lack of feeling, the cast did.

When Clive Barnes did show up, January 30, 1969,

the performance was bad. We had worked our asses off, but it hurt us. We were too tired. The hassles over whether or not Gerry and Jim should do the show wore us out. Everybody made mistakes during the performance: lines and cues were blown; Melba, one of the most consistent soloists, went blank, and worst of all, the band screwed up.

For a confusing fifteen seconds during the Be-In, the cast was singing and dancing to "Hare Krishna" while the band was playing "Love Love." At first none of us could believe it, but we finally got it together.

The cast was confident that Clive Barnes would give the show a bad review, but he didn't. He still urged people to go and see *Hair*.

38

Booze was never a thing with the original Broadway cast. But when new people joined the show, booze-heads started popping up. Spotting one was easy—slurred speech, staggering, the smell of Listerine-over-booze on the breath.

I only knew one guy whose job was threatened because of his drinking. During one performance he fell asleep onstage, and I had to wake him up so he could say his lines. At another, he was so high he could hardly talk. He sang his solo leaning over like the Tower of Pisa. After the dismissal threat, he cooled it.

Erik Robinson kept a bottle of Southern Comfort in his dressing-room-table drawer. He nipped frequently before, during, and after the show. "I like drinking a little wine or whiskey so I can relax. I used to drink about a pint of Southern Comfort a performance. On matinee days, about a fifth to a quart."

One day, though, Erik said he decided not to drink at all. He felt relaxed enough to go on without it.

As Claude, Erik sang "Where Do I Go?," walking from stage left to stage center before backing up to climb the platform. "I always tried to perfect the song, to sing better each time," he said. "That night I was perfectly straight."

All the lights dimmed. The spotlight zoomed in on him, as he began to walk from stage left to stage center. Then he was gone.

"Somehow, I walked right off the front of the stage and fell into the lap of a man in the audience.

"He looked at me. I looked at him. It seemed like the stage had simply disappeared," Erik said. "Fortunately no one was hurt. The man didn't know if it was part of the show or not. He couldn't believe I was sitting in his lap, still singing. I didn't drop a single word of the song."

The spotlight roamed around the stage in search of Erik until he finally reappeared, bolstered by two people from the audience.

As Claude, Erik was often late returning onstage for the draft-card-burning scene. He had to wash off the mud from the tar and feather scene first. But at one particular performance it wasn't the mud or the Southern Comfort that was detaining him.

Erik usually took a shower, then ran back upstairs

to his dressing room naked. One or two of the dressers would be waiting to help him put on his costume and make it back in time for his next cue.

Sally Eaton was in the dressing room while he was going through his quick-change act.

"I stood there, naked and spreadeagled, waiting to be dressed," Erik said. "The next thing I knew Sally was saying, 'Oh, what a beautiful cock you have,' and her mouth was on it. She was down on her knees giving me head.

"The first time I was amazed, because she was so candid about the whole thing. [Erik was very new to the show at this time.] I mean nothing stopped her. Nothing seemed to stop the dressers from doing their jobs either. Somehow I was getting clothes put on me and being sucked off at the same time."

Charles O. Lynch said he could see Sally and Erik behind him in the mirror as he was putting on his make-up for the Margaret Mead number. Evidently Sally could not bear to see Erik standing around bare-assed. She'd grab at him, and he'd slap her hands, saying "Sally, come on. Sally, stop. Don't. I'm going to be late."

This happened every night.

"I slapped on my powers to try to ignore it," Charles said, "but the one that had me putting lipstick on my nose was Barry McGuire's cock impressions."

The first time Charles saw it, he couldn't believe his near-sighted eyes. He couldn't see too well without his glasses and he had to crane his neck to get a better view through the dressing room mirrors.

Finally, he said to himself, "Let me just see what's happening," and put his glasses on. By that time the cock impression game was nearly over.

A few nights later he asked Sally and Barry to repeat the whole thing for him. He told me it was one of the funniest things he'd ever seen.

Barry McGuire played a game with his cock which was a series of impressions that he or she, or both of them, could make with it.

Barry would take his balls—"he had the heavy, loose kind"—and stretch them over his cock—"which was soft"—so that just the head peeked out. That was called "The Shy Turtle."

Then he'd tuck his cock behind his balls and put the balls around his cock. This was called "Half a Grapefruit."

Then he'd hold the base of his cock and stretch it around his third finger so that it looked like a ring. This was called "The Wide Wedding Band."

Then he'd tuck his cock and balls in between his legs so that nothing but his pubic hair showed. This, he said, was "A two-hundred-and-fifty-pound dyke."

His last was to take the head of his cock and stretch the opening back so that it looked like lips. This was "Al Jolson Singing 'Swanee.' (Or 'Mammy')."

Everyone who saw it said it was hysterical. When Barry demonstrated his cock impressions to Fred Rheinglas, Fred cracked up.

"Can you top that?" he asked Sally.

"Of course, I can't pick up a coin with my pussy or anything like that," Sally told me.

It was hard to figure Sally out. She was one of the few people in the cast who stuck up for management the majority of the time. I think she thought that might protect her from being fired.

I always tried to tell her, "When they get tired of

you, they're just going to fire you like they do everybody else."

"No, they won't," she'd say. "They're not going to fire me." Unless something happened to directly affect her, she was usually on management's side.

Sally was one of the last people from the original company to be fired. The Miss America Contest has its Miss Congeniality award, *Hair* should have given one for "Consistency in Performance" to Sally. She deserved it.

I had always wanted to play Jeanie, the pregnant girl who sings about "Air" pollution. Sally played the part and Suzannah Norstrand was first understudy. When Suzannah left I went from second to first understudy. One night I went on in the role. Although I felt unprepared, I decided to do it anyway. "But," I told the stage manager, "I'll take the script with me." Onstage I never had to refer to it, but the fact that I had the script cracked up the audience.

When Sally heard I was good as Jeanie, her absences from the show decreased sharply. One day she even tried to give me notes on her interpretation of Jeanie, on how it should be done. She bugged me about it, but I ignored her. Everybody brings their own thing to a part. Sally had hers and I had mine. Admittedly, out of all the different Jeanies I had ever seen, none were better than Sally's.

Charles O. Lynch told me about the time Sally wandered backstage crying, "I want to get out of here so badly. I can't stand it any longer." Charles said he felt sorry for her, but he didn't want to get too involved. He asked her why she didn't leave.

Apparently the question triggered something in her, because Sally turned on the tears and gave him a long rendition of herself, which concluded: "What else can I do?"

"That's just it," Charles said. "What else could she do?"

Charles told me that he later showed her an article in a trade paper describing a role in *The Owl and The Pussycat*.

"Hey, Sally," he said, "why don't you follow this up?"

She looked at the paper, then said, "No, I couldn't do that."

"Why not?"

"Because," she said, "they say she's a 'bubble-gum-chewing type hippie,' and I'm not that kind of hippie."

One Saturday evening, as Charles O. Lynch was returning to the theater, he passed Sally's dressing room and saw she was nude from the waist up. That was not unusual, he said, but she was wearing high-heeled black leather boots, and that was.

"She asked me how I liked it," Charles said.

Then he noticed that she was wearing some kind of leather jock-strap with silver studs on it. "The genital area was stuffed like a Shakespearean cod piece."

He told her that "it" looked fine, but what was "it" for?

"I'm going to an S and M party," she said.

Charles was so naive he assumed "S and M" meant stage manager. "The initials 'S' and 'M' have always meant stage manager to me." She told him it was a Sado-Masochist party.

"I had nothing more to say and decided to move on, fast. Then suddenly, she grabbed her left breast and squirted me in the face with mother's milk."

Someone once told me that after Sally was fired she used to walk around the streets, dressed in her Jeanie costume.

I wasn't really surprised. She wasn't the only one who was shook up by *Hair*.

Erik Robinson joined the New York cast when Gerry and Jim returned from doing the L.A. gig. After doing the show for about six or seven months, he requested time off from management to get rid of a cold. They refused.

Erik, who was playing Claude, repeatedly asked the propmen to mix the mud for the tar and feather scene with hot water because he had caught cold and gotten laryngitis.

The propmen told him that would be a hassle. Translation: they wouldn't have time to go around the corner to the Haymarket for a drink. To save time "they used to mix up the mud ahead of time."

Erik volunteered to mix it himself. He was told that "the props are only to be handled by propmen."

There was also a hassle with other props used by Claude—newspapers. Some nights they were there, other nights they weren't. When Erik told the propmen he would take care of the newspapers himself, they said, "You can't touch the props. Now, how many times do we have to tell you?"

"It got to be a thing," Erik said. "I complained to management all the time. Nothing ever seemed to be done about it."

Erik wrote management, requesting that they either grant him a two-week vacation or they accept his two-week notice. An Equity rule states that actors aren't due vacations until they've been with a show a year, but most of the cast took their vacations before the year was up because otherwise we couldn't stand the pace. If you were an absentee, it was cool; but if you never missed a performance, it was rough.

Erik got a telegram back from Michael Butler saying that his resignation had been accepted.

"I continued as if nothing had happened. It still upset me that the mud was cold and the newspapers were missing when I needed them." And he still complained about it to management.

"One night, after the cold mud was plastered all over my body," Erik said, "I picked up the bucket and threw it at the propmen backstage. . . . I wasn't going to stand for it anymore. Throughout the rest of the performance I did other goofy things."

Afterwards, the assistant director, Glen Nielson, accused Erik of being "terribly unprofessional." In a show like *Hair* you were professional if you *showed* up. Glen told Erik that other people agreed with him, and that Erik should get himself together.

"I was too upset to hassle with him anymore. I went to the dressing room, hoping I would find some kind of solace or friendship. When Heather MacRae and Oatis Stephens, two people I was very close to, said, 'You did act a little unprofessional,' that did it. If they thought so, too, then it must be true. I sunk lower than down. I thought it must be the end. There was nothing here for me anymore. It was dead and gone. I started to get angry that I'd spent all this time in a dead thing."

Erik short-circuited. He went upstairs and locked himself in the bathroom. "If I didn't, I'd probably beat the shit out of Oatis, or somebody else. I totally demolished the john, literally tearing things out of the concrete. The adrenalin in my veins made me into a superman."

I was coming off stage when I heard Erik crying and screaming in the locked john, smashing things. By the time I got upstairs, some of the cast and stage managers were banging on the door, yelling "Come out of there!" A few of the cast were standing on the stairway, crying.

I told everyone to shut up. You don't have to be a genius to see that adding hysteria to hysteria will not solve the problem.

"Get away from that door," I said, my voice lowered. They split apart.

After the yelling had ceased and everyone went away, I leaned against the door and said, "Erik, this is Mary Davis," then talked to him in as normal a voice as possible. He began to quiet down and started whimpering. He said I could talk to him in the john if I came in alone.

The bathroom was in a bad way; so was he. His face and eyes were almost purple. His nose was running. His hair and clothes were disheveled. He was still so excited that I had to calm him down, like consoling a child, before I could talk to him.

I convinced Erik to leave the john and go get freshened up. We left the theater with another guy in the cast, who put him up in his place for a while. Erik did only two more shows after that, then left New York to get his head together. He said it took him three months.

39

Management gave the cast a party backstage for our first *Hair* birthday with decorations and the usual refreshments.

It was May, 1969, and the show was falling apart. Most of the original cast had gone; a lot of new people had come. The party was hanging by its nails when, suddenly, there was a big commotion near Fred Rheinglas.

Erroll Addison Booker was having a confrontation with Bob Chapman, who had been talking to Fred. Chapman is about six-and-a-half-feet tall, a good head taller than Erroll, who is six foot himself. Erroll caught Bob when he was "looking the other way."

"I caught him with one of those running punches that comes up from off the ground and laid it behind his ears. From then on, I was on his ass. I knew he hadn't done too much fisticuffs in his life. He was trying to get away. He got out from under Fred, then I climbed over Fred, and about five stagehands pulled me off Bob."

Everybody had thought that Erroll and Steve Curry, who came to the party, had jumped Chapman.

"Steve Curry had jumped in when the stagehands were messing with me," Erroll said. "Curry was going to run up and hit Bob, but he checked out how big he was and changed his mind. Then Joe Cavallaro grabbed Curry. Curry got mad and kicked him. Meanwhile, Chapman ran to the back of the theater saying to Michael Butler, "You got to give me police protection."

"Joe Cavallaro, my manager, was there with his lawyer," Erroll said. "Joe was going to hit Bob. I said, 'No, let me hit him.' I took off my clogs and went to his ass."

Things in the show were so bad that Michael Butler decided to throw in another trip to Fire Island and pay for dinner.

The cast went out on a Saturday night, right after the show. I was so tired I flaked out on the bus. It didn't matter. The whole trip was really broken down this time. Nothing was happening between people in the cast, so nothing was happening with the cast. This last-gasp attempt to recapture the original "tribal" spirit dissipated into a complete farce.

It was the third and last trip to Fire Island that I knew of.

"The honeymoon," as Tom O'Horgan once said, "was over."

Julie Arenal felt that management did two things wrong. One was the Good Doctor, the other was saying the show was nothing but love. "If you're telling kids you are not in a business and love is the only thing that counts, as I've heard the director tell them, it's BULLSHIT!

"The kids in the show weren't pretending," Julie said. "They were as hip as could be, but some of them went under with the feeling of 'What if you don't love?' The whole hippie movement wanted it to be just that way." And so, we thought, did "the chief of the tribe."

Michael Butler stopped coming around soon after Fire Island trip number three. He sent his messages to us by telex instead. Sometimes the best indicator of what was happening with our "chief" was what you read in the newspapers and magazines.

"This is a hard show to run," Michael Butler explained to a *Life* magazine journalist.* "It's all right for the kids to bring up basic employee problems. But if you want to oppose them with basic business rules, they're ready to throw the whole hippie philosophy of love at you."

We still had tribal meetings, however. We had to go to the stage managers with our problems, who, more often than not, were the cause of the problems to begin with. At any rate, they never knew how to handle it.

I heard that there were unofficial tribal meetings with the "chief" up in his "tower," as some of the cast referred to his penthouse apartment. I never went to any of those, but a few members of the tribe did.

One girl in the cast, who had been to one such session, told me that Michael Butler and his cronies met with half a dozen or so of the cast about "what to do about the show?" She said that the tribal meetings "up at the palace" were like "ego-trip chats." Some of the cast fostered a hope of "keeping the tribe together." They had a plan to "do a number on Michael Butler" by taking *Hair* around the country on an "underground" road tour without telling management about it.

*Josh Greenfeld, June 27, 1969

Nothing ever happened. It was just another symptom of discontent. Many of them were talking about leaving at that point.

By July of 1969 the turnover in *Hair* was so rapid that management got a brainstorm of an idea for updating the pictures in the display cases in front of the theater.

They sent the entire cast—all thirty of us—to the Passport Photo Shop to have our pictures taken. Then the individual head shots were blown up to 8 by 10 glossies. They weren't too bad, and they provided management with instant replacement photos for the lightning cast turnover. The pictures often were outdated the moment they were hung.

One time a guy in the show approached me and said, "Hello, my name is Singer Williams."

"Honey," I said, "I've seen them come and I've seen them go. When you've been here for a week, you come back and tell me what your name is. I'll be glad to talk to you then."

In August, there was a big house-cleaning. Nine or more of the cast were fired in one fell swoop. Most of them, including Erroll Addison Booker, had participated in a nude strike.

40

Upstaging was everyone's thing. The kids in the cast with experience were the ones who worried most about how big or small their parts were. They also knew how to maneuver themselves onstage. Two cast members in particular, Paul Jabara and Natalie Mosco, were always trying to get up-front. I felt it at rehearsals but I picked up on this a few months after we'd opened, when, at my request, I saw the show as a member of the audience for the first time.

I figured if they're going to do it, so am I. No one wanted to be in the background. First come, first seen. "There's a little bit of Eve Harrington in everyone," said Jonathan Kramer, referring to the ambitious ingenue in *All About Eve*. I always felt I had to be one step ahead of all the other "Eves" onstage.

Once, while I was reciting the Gettysberg Address as Abe, Jonathan, who was chewing bubble gum, was working hard on blowing a big bubble. I was unaware of it until I heard laughter from the audience. Without dropping a line, I broke the bubble right in his face. He just stood there with the gum hanging from his chin while the audience applauded.

But upstaging really reached its peak in the nude scene. After all the initial timidity about stripping, almost everyone reached the point of practically fighting to get the best spot.

Many of the girls were so anxious to strip they didn't even take time off while they were menstruating, and we and the audience were treated to the sight of hanging tampon strings. Many of the cast also used attention-getting devices, gimmicks and tricks, such as painting small, Day-Glo or florescent figures around their navels or anywhere else on their bodies. Gerry had been known to paint his genitals different colors. Some stuck sequins or glittering pieces of jewelry to themselves; others held bunches of wildly colored flowers, or coupled off and held hands.

Technically Sally Eaton should not have been in the nude scene, since Jeanie was supposed to be pregnant. After Sally had her baby, she wore a fake stomach, which she'd take off to do the nude scene.

"After I did the nude scene for a while I really dug it," Erroll Addison Booker said. "I used to tie rags around myself. It was a total goof to be able to stand up in front of thousands of folks with their field and opera glasses pinned on you."

"I used to do the whole show with a bowtie and ripped-up rags," said Robert I. "For the nude scene I'd take off all my clothes except for the bowtie. The kids said, if you don't stop doing it, we're going on strike. Shelly was the spokesman. They didn't like people making fun of the nude scene. It was like something they considered sacred."

At one particularly heated tribal meeting, Jonathan Kramer said to the chief, "You're making a fortune off my naked ass, and I want some money for it. That's what's dragging the people into the theater."

We knew management had once considered bringing in ringers who would have been paid to strip. For the cast, management came up with the insulting figure of $1.50 per strip per person. John said it was like extraordinary risk money. "For free was exploitation; for $1.50 we were selling our asses cheap. Hookers made more than we did."

But some of the cast felt it was an added bonus. Personally, I felt the whole idea of paying us to strip was trashy. Paul Jabara said he stood up one night and flashed just his naked ass to the audience. He got paid 75 cents for it.

I stripped only when I felt turned on by good vibes from the audience or the cast. And occasionally, I stripped for those unknown but beautiful men in the audience.

After a year and a half, many of the cast decided that $1.50 per strip wasn't enough. A lot of the guys, especially, felt it was unfair. "It bothered me that we only got paid $1.50," Erroll said. "I knew that's what was packing the house."

They approached Bill Orton, the business manager, with their complaint, but he refused to give them a raise. The nudes decided to go on strike. I tried to tell them that a strike was not the way. The cast had never stuck together for any one thing before, and they weren't about to now.

The first night of the nude strike all but one cast member refrained from doing the nude scene. This went on for three or four performances. Melba Moore, who continued to do the nude scene, simply didn't agree with the others.

Most of the problem stemmed from our contracts. The original cast had nothing at all in their contracts about doing a nude scene. The new cast members' contracts, however, had riders attached, stating: "The actor agrees to appear nude in 'The Nude Scene' at the end of Act I."

New cast members claimed that, regardless of any rider in their contracts, management assured them they wouldn't have to do the nude scene if they didn't want to.

When my contract came up for renewal, Bill Orton said, "You know, you don't have to strip if you don't want to," then waited for me to sign the nude clause.

"If I don't have to strip, remove the clause from my contract." It was deleted.

When the nudes went on strike, management put the screws on those striking members who had signed the nude-scene rider in their contracts. They were told they'd be fired or brought up on charges of breach of contract before Equity.

Eventually the strikers gave in. The price of a strip remained at $1.50.

I stopped stripping altogether, because too many people in the audience were sneaking in cameras and taking pictures. Management attempted to stop it by removing the film from the camera if they caught an offender. But then why were there nude-scene pictures in the souvenir book sold in the lobby, in the New York *Times* magazine section, and in private collections? Jonathan Kramer told me that he saw a picture of me nude in the English newspapers while he was in England.

The cast had many offers to pose nude for money, either individually or in groups, which was O.K. if that was their thing. It wasn't mine.

41

Despite the propaganda to the contrary, undertones of racial inequality were always present in *Hair*.

In the early part of the run it all looked good up front. The interchangeability of roles between the sexes—"we are all equal"—as well as races—"there are no black and white parts in the show"—made *Hair* look totally integrated. And, I must admit, most of the singing roles were carried by the black cast.

But when the original cast started to leave, and their replacements left a lot to be desired, we began to wonder why blacks weren't being given a chance to do larger parts, like leading roles.

Only bit parts* were being racially interchanged, not major roles like Claude, Berger, Sheila, Jeanie. That didn't come till a full year later.

Ben Vereen, the first black Broadway Berger, was fired after about two weeks. As I mentioned earlier, he was considered by many to be as good as Gerry, who was the best Berger.

When Heather MacRae left the show, the desperate

---

* Roles such as the Principals and Mother and Father were considered bit parts. Nondescript roles such as Buddhist priests, nuns, green berets, etc., were chorus spots which were cast free-for-alls. Anyone could play any of them.

search to find someone to replace her was called "the Sheila Sweepstakes." After trying out nearly all the white girls, management finally gave the part to a black girl who had the best voice in the show—Melba Moore.

George Tipton, a black guy in the cast, told me that he didn't think there was "any more of a racial problem in the show than there is outside of the show."

On the same subject, Erroll Addison Booker came down a bit more heavy: "They really capitalized off niggers. I mean the voices, the humor, the beauty. They had all the studs ... they had the whole thing. They had us there shuffling like motherfuckers, and it was a valid art form."

Undoubtedly, *Hair* opened up jobs for black performers on Broadway who otherwise might not have gotten there. For myself, until *Hair,* most shows wanted legitimate voices, the typical Broadway musical sound. The black sound, mine, was not accepted then.

Virnette Carroll, director of the statewide Ghetto Arts Programs, said in the *Amsterdam News*: "Surely *Hair* is the first truly integrated Broadway musical, as much because of the way the talents of the blacks in the show are employed as because of the fact of their employment."*

Our "truly integrated show" was just another *Hair* rip-off, but we didn't see it until incidents unravelled, slowly, like a snag in a sweater.

What happened after Lamont Washington died speaks for itself, especially in view of the fact that one year later, Michael Butler closed the San Francisco show so that the cast of *Hair* could watch him play polo in Los Angeles.

*July 20, 1968

At one time the black cast called a meeting among themselves and decided to face management with charges of prejudice. Before we could get our case together management underwent dramatic staff changes and we were told Michael Butler could not be reached. Many of us could not help but wonder why the death of Martin Luther King never had been acknowledged, when a Sunday matinee and night show were cancelled out of respect for the death of Bobby Kennedy. And, outside of the cast and the band, why weren't there more black people within the *Hair* organization?

During my time with the show I noticed one black girl in the *Hair* office and three black assistant stage managers. Donnie Burks was a second assistant stage manager, then Bob Chapman was offered the job of assistant stage manager to induce him to remain with the show. Bob was eventually replaced by David Paine on the board side and Erroll Addison Booker on the cast side. When asked, Erroll refused to be assistant stage manager. Giving that job to a black was like "a kiss of death," he said. Whoever got it was either fired shortly thereafter or on his way out. The theater porter was black, however.

When *Playbill** published an article on *Hair* with photographs, not one black cast member was represented; but when the *Soul* show, a black oriented TV program, requested black kids *only,* Michael Butler sent the stage manager around with a message: the black cast members do *not* represent the entire show, and if the group is not integrated no one will be allowed to go on.

None of the black cast—Melba, Emmeretta, Ronnie, Erroll, Leata, Donnie, Jim Fields, or myself—was against

*September 1968

integrating, but when I pointed out examples of white segregation in the show, nobody knew anything. Much later a cast member told me that someone high in management had a thing about blacks and whites being photographed together.

We did the *Soul* show black and white.

When the four white students at Kent State University were killed on May 4, 1970, we were all outraged. In their honor, by order of management, the cast was requested not to bring the audience onstage at the end of the show but to ask them to join us instead in a moment of silence. The cast and the audience gladly partook of the tribute.

A few weeks later, on May 14, three black students at Jackson State College were killed. The first day the news broke, the production stage manager, Bob Currie, claimed no knowledge of the incident. A few of the cast, black and white, stood in silence for a few minutes that night while the rest, including the audience, danced around us. At the next performance I again asked the production stage manager if he'd heard from management whether we could pay "a moment of silence" tribute to the dead Jackson college students.

"You can do it if you want to," he said. "I haven't heard anything from management." The entire cast joined in the moment of silence that night.

Danny Sullivan, acting director, once said, "*Hair* is talking about the power to be human beings, not black or white power, but it doesn't come across in the show. My objection to the black thing in *Hair* is that the black man's being used for his blackness.

"Most of the kids in the show are display hippies—the

niggers of the hippie movement—and *Hair* is pandering to boffo land."

I had to laugh. "Why do you [whites] always take what we have? We can't even be niggers anymore."

I knew one thing. All of us believed in the good things the show had to say. For the original cast, *Hair* became a crusade. Freedom, the underlying message of *Hair,* has been the message of blacks for years, only nobody (the white masses) ever listened to us. At first we had hoped that the Gospel According to *Hair* would spread from the company to the audiences who thronged to see it.

When the shit hit the fan, I tried to get what little black message there was across with the part of Hud, and also my own part, Abie.

"You were the first bit of black power on Broadway when you did your Abe Lincoln number," said Jonathan Kramer. "You were the first one to hit those honkies on the head with pure black ass."

Some of the audience would get really riled when, as Abe I pushed over the "shoeshine boy" (played by a white girl) with my foot, commenting that the quality of shoeshine boys was on the decline. Their eyes would flash looks of anger which would follow me throughout the rest of the show.

"If you say it like Aunt Jemima," Erroll said, "it's O.K. But when you run it down like it is, they don't want to hear it. It's no longer funny."

42

One day, while watching Danny Sullivan put the cast through the same tiresome, tedious sensory exercises, I wondered, "What *am* I doing here?" There seemed to be absolutely no sense in having people, who didn't want to do so, touch each other out of "love." The show and everything it had to say had become a travesty. Just like the Haight-Ashbury had become a burial ground for the flower children, so *Hair* had become a mausoleum for the "Sunshine" kids.

Nobody was really into the exercises or each other. They were like automatons going through the motions because someone had pushed the button. I was in a bad place and I knew it. I got an attitude. If the exercises involved only one other person, I bowed out. If it was a group effort, I took part, half-heartedly.

Danny caught me glaring at him at one point. We had a few words, then he suggested that we go to the back of the theater to talk.

"What's the matter with you?" he asked. "I don't like the way you've been acting. I know you're upset about Melba. . . ." He was referring to Melba being fired.

Ever since Melba had won the "Sheila Sweepstakes," the intramural jealousy among the girls in the cast had intensified. Many of the black girls were involved, too. At first I had my doubts about Melba playing Sheila. I was surprised when she turned out to be good, and told her so. No one could beat Melba for singing. (Once when Lynn Kellogg left the show in the fall of 1968, Galt had asked me to audition for the part. I didn't get it. At the audition, the song, "Easy To Be Hard," was too high for me, but they didn't want to lower the key.) Melba was vocally one hundred percent better than any of the girls in the show, black or white, at the time, but resentment backstage was rife, and eventually most of the girls in the cast stopped speaking to her out of jealousy. The guys didn't care one way or another.

Melba was fresh and vibrant when she first played Sheila. The band really played their asses off when she sang "Good Morning Starshine." I heard flutes and horns I didn't even know were there. They really cooked. After a couple of weeks, the singing was still fabulous but I felt she was doing stick as far as acting went.

Melba was still playing Sheila when she gave her two-week notice. She was taking a vacation and then going on to do *Purlie*. But she never did the last week. Apparently, Danny Sullivan had told her she was just "walking through the part," and not to bother to come in. Some of us felt very down about it. Maybe Melba was lame-ducking a bit, but she was an original cast member who had been with the show for about eighteen months. Even sleep-walking through the part of Sheila, she was better than the understudy.

The understudy was so bad that once, while she was singing "Easy To Be Hard," one of the musicians threw down his instrument in disgust. He said he wouldn't play for her anymore because she couldn't sing. It's a quiet song, and I was certain she must have heard him. I felt embarrassed for her but agreed with him.

Most of the black girls in the cast were glad to see Melba go. But I thought that instead of bad-mouthing Melba they should have been glad to see another black making it. Backstage was degenerating from ego-tripping into out-and-out throat-cutting. I just didn't like it.

After Melba left, her understudy didn't speak to me for months, which gave me a chance to cool off.* Now I just had to contend with the building hostility I felt toward Danny.

Since he had brought up Melba during our argument in the back of the theater, I followed through. I told him I didn't like the way he treated Melba; that he must be aware of the rumor going around that he had fired her for his own special reason.

He was furious. He told me to go home and stay there if I didn't want to take part in the rehearsals.

He was right, except that he was bothering me far more than the chaotic show or useless rehearsals. That, I was used to. I just got so sick of management preaching "love" and "equality" at their convenience. What's wrong is wrong. I wasn't tired of doing *Hair,* I was tired of the same persistent lies, the same old propaganda that they were still trying to shove down our throats.

*As soon as Melba became a hit in *Purlie,* those who had previously bad-mouthed her suddenly turned into back-patters.

43

Gerry, Jim, a few others, and I were sitting in Joe Allen's one night.

"I've been thinking about writing a book about *Hair*," I said. The idea had first occurred to me during the television talk shows, when everyone wanted to know what being in *Hair* was really like. Lamont's death clinched it: I would try to answer the question.

Gerry and Jim became very enthusiastic. Gerry suggested I tape my interviews and said he would even buy me a tape recorder. I thought he was kidding and forgot about it.

A couple of days later the doorman at the theater told me there was a package in my name. I was really floored when I saw what it was—a brand new Sony tape recorder. Gerry also suggested that I interview all the *Hair* companies. I had met people from many other companies, and every one of them wanted to see it all hang out.

Both Gerry and Jim knew I wanted to interview them. One of my very first interviews was with Jim, squeezed in between a rehearsal and a show. Though I only asked general questions about Gerry's and his relationship with the cast, we soon went off on irrelevant tangents. I thought he was evasive. Jim always gave me the impression he was afraid of what I was going to say next anyway. He promised me another interview later.

After I interviewed Jim, one of *Hair*'s P.R. people approached me.

"I heard that you're writing a book about *Hair*," Michael Gifford said. "Aren't you afraid that something might happen to you?"

If it was an attempt to intimidate me, it didn't work.

In the meantime, I started to interview everyone who had anything to do with the production of *Hair*. When Gerry and Jim saw that I was really serious, they became harder and harder to pin down for an interview. After a few months of hedging, they suggested I write out questions and submit the list to their manager.

I made up a list of twenty-seven questions. The most intimate ones were: "Were you always hippies?" and "How have your lives changed since the success of *Hair*?" I even attached a note specifying that they only had to answer the questions they wanted.

The next time I saw them I asked if they had received the questions. They made up excuses about thinking up answers. I finally gave up the idea of interviewing them.

When Michael Butler heard I was writing a book, he sent a telegram to Lani Ball, the stage manager: "Is this our Mary Davis? Ask Michael Gifford. I will do anything I can."

He seemed pleased when I asked him for an interview.

After many calls and messages about setting up the time and place, Michael Butler's representative in

Chicago, Cary King, made an appointment for me to see Michael on Sunday, October 12, 1969, at his home in Oak Brook, Illinois. The chief of the tribe was, in fact, giving a party for the Chicago *Hair* cast that day.

I took my vacation and I flew out to Chicago three days early on my own time and money, thinking I could combine business with pleasure. But reading the Chicago *News* on the plane en route, I learned about the police riots going on in the Windy City. That killed my tourist plans.

I went to the Chicago *Hair* office to tell them I had arrived and Cary King reaffirmed my appointment with Michael Butler.

Since the city looked like a police state, I hung around the *Hair* theater or my hotel for the next three days. Cops were everywhere, guarding buildings, lined up in the streets. From my hotel room I could see bands of people marching through the streets. There were rumors of beatings, killings, burnings, blow-ups. Only my interview with Michael Butler kept me from leaving Chicago right then.

The Chicago production of *Hair* gave its first preview on Saturday. I thought it was a shitty performance, lackluster. Clive Barnes' reviews of the official opening were glowing.

Claude has a line in the play about giving the pill to Mayor Daley. The New York Claude at the time had told me he had received a· letter from Michael Butler asking him to strike the line until the opening of the Chicago show, so as "not to offend the good mayor." As far as the New York and Chicago shows went, the "good mayor" was not "offended": the line was struck for the time being.

I searched for Michael Butler at the theater that night without any luck. He wasn't expected, Chicago management told me, and also his party scheduled for Sunday had been cancelled.

Bertrand Castelli gave me Michael Butler's Oak Brook number, which I called to confirm our interview. I left a message with his answering service. Michael Butler's answering service and I got to know each other pretty well before I left Chicago. His lack of response to my calls didn't shake me up too much. I already knew that Big Chief spake with Forked Tongue.

Two days after my return to New York, I got a letter from Michael Butler: "What happened to you? I tried to reach you several times. I am sorry we were not able to get together. I've heard some unpleasant things that you've said about me, and therefore, I would have welcomed meeting you. Peace. . . ."

Okay, I thought, we'll play it his way. After receiving his letter, I tried to call his Oak Brook home long distance twice more only to renew my rapport with his answering service. That failing, I wrote him a letter. A few days later I got back my air-mail-special-delivery, registered-receipt-requested letter, unclaimed.

The next time I saw Michael Butler neither one of us brought the incident up. Why bother?

44

For *Hair*'s second birthday, April, 1970, management planned to give a free *Hair* concert in Central Park. Our private little "birthday" celebrations were becoming public sensations. Afterwards a dinner party was planned at the Four Seasons restaurant for cast, management, and friends of management.

The publicity machine was set in motion and invitations were sent out. The front of the card consisted of a picture of the entire cast standing onstage nude behind a banner which said, "What Else Would You Wear On Your Second Birthday!"

Some of the kids, mostly the guys, actually were nude behind the banner. A few of the girls and I wore our underwear, pulling down our bra straps so that they wouldn't show. The picture looked authentic. There we were, twenty-four naked, happy "hippies" inviting you to join us. It was an obvious come-on. Management had finally resorted to openly exploiting nudity as a main draw. It took them a while to do it, but by then they certainly couldn't have sold the show on talent.

Hair's free concert in the park took place on a sunny Sunday. As the cast got ready for its procession entry, I dug the audience: people as far as the eye could see. Nearly ten thousand of them, I later read. For our opening number we sang "Happy Birthday" to ourselves, enjoining the audience to sing with us. Oliver, who had made a hit recording of "Good Morning Starshine," was there to sing his version of the song. Oatis Stephens and Heather MacRae, who were no longer with the show, sang "Rocky Raccoon" as a duet. Shelley Winters publicly wished the cast a happy birthday.

The audience seemed to dig us, but it wasn't until the cast sang the finale, "Let the Sunshine In," that they really reacted as a crowd. *Hair* had to be one of America's most successful musicals. The audience looked like one gigantic *Hair* groupie out there, standing, waving, cheering, singing, flashing the "V" sign. For a minute I almost believed the *Hair* philosophy had gotten through. It was just a rush, nice while it lasted.

From the vases lining the stage Gerry threw flowers, and when they were gone, water. No one seemed to mind. The people sitting closest to the stage were mostly backers, and for $310,000 a week in returns at this point, Gerry could dump one of the Great Lakes on them.

After the concert, everyone who had been invited—and some who hadn't—wandered down to the Four Seasons.

My boyfriend Tom and I went down to the restaurant to check if I had time to run home to change. I had bought a beautiful silver velour dress from Saks Fifth Avenue especially for the party. Nearly everyone was dressed in varying styles of dressy hippie drag, but I wanted to wear something sexy and glamorous for a change.

There were groups of hippies picketing outside the Four Seasons. They demanded that the restaurant give them $100,000 for the Panther Defense Fund, that *Hair* give a percentage of its gross to help stop the Vietnam war, or to help the poor, and so on. I even heard some of them demand dinner.

Tom waited for me at the restaurant while I raced home. When I returned, the police had already taken thirteen protestors, including Jim Rado, to jail. It was reported that pot was smoked inside the paddy-wagon and nine of them, again including Jim, spent the night in jail.

He certainly didn't miss much at the Four Seasons. Aside from the cast, some of whom were wading barefoot in the restaurant's fountain pools, the dinner party was full of members of what we called the *Hair* confederacy—money people and promoters—all sitting at Michael Butler's table.

From a free concert in the park to an expensive Establishment restaurant—that just about summed up the two heads of *Hair* for me.

45

When Cliff Lipson, the cast dance captain, left *Hair* to do *Jesus Christ Superstar,* management decided to make me dance captain. I suspected they gave me the job to pacify me and to keep me in the show. Besides playing one of the strongest parts, Abie, who else could take on the job? Who knew the steps? It also paid an extra fifty dollars a week.

I was optimistic enough to think it would put me in a better position to help pull the show back together. I was in *Hair* when it was good; I still didn't want to see it die.

One of the dance captain's responsibilities is to help train new people. There was no real authority behind the job so trying to get something accomplished was hard. Lack of cooperation from either management or the cast made it next to impossible.

The cast of *Hair* at the time was the absolute worst I had ever seen. I couldn't even imagine what criteria they were using for auditions. And the less talent someone had, the more difficult he or she was to handle. Few of the present cast spoke or related to each other either onstage or off. Communication was at its worst. Everyone wanted to do everything his or her own way.

There was one girl in particular who was the sickest person I've ever worked with outside of a nursing situation. She seldom spoke to people, and when she did it was in anger. You couldn't say anything without setting off a tantrum. No matter what I said she would take it personally and go into her bag. Her boyfriend was also in the show, and they used to argue constantly. He would sometimes tell the rest of the cast not to pay any attention to her.

As dance captain I had to try to coach her, but no matter what approach I took, she wouldn't listen. If I tried to make something simple, she accused me of treating her like a baby. If I spoke to her officially, as the dance captain, she said I was bossing her around. If I tried to give her notes about her dancing, she claimed I was picking on her. Nothing I did worked.

One day, thinking I had been talking about her, she threatened to punch me in the mouth in front of four very surprised people, including myself. I told her as nicely as possible that she was badly in need of medical attention, and I would be glad to recommend someone. She left the room crying.

I needed help with the situation. I went to Bob Currie, the production stage manager, and explained the problem to him.

"You're going to have to find a way to deal with her yourself," he told me. Ditto from Danny Sullivan. Part of his job as stage manager was to tell this girl to either shape up or ship out. He never hesitated to tell me when he thought I needed to hear it. At least he put us in different dressing rooms.

Nevertheless, things got worse. While onstage one day, she did punch me during a dance number. I was so surprised I didn't retaliate, but I told Danny Sullivan and also Bob Currie about it. She denied the whole thing. Nothing was done.

I knew my time was up at *Hair*, that I had to get out. The kids now in the show were being used to sell the show. The drug situation was worse than ever, with some of management's conduct questionable; most of the cast and management didn't care about the quality of the show but only basked in their association with it; the self-appointed "chief" was becoming more and more overwhelmed with status and position in the very Establishment he once wanted to tear down; communication backstage was nil; even doing the material wasn't enough for me anymore. The pressure of trying to care in the face of such indifference finally was beginning to get to me. I'd had all the nuts I could take.

46

With the exception of Actors' Fund benefits, most of the benefits we did turned into public relations fuel for management and just another hassle for us. They were badly rehearsed, disorganized performances which transformed the cast into a pack of fumbling upstagers. Early in the game I announced I'd had it with the benefit shit and refused to do any unless they were rehearsed and we were paid for them. When you're doing something for free, most of the time the audience is very hard on you. That bothered me even more than not being paid, especially in view of the bad benefit performances we usually gave.

One exception was the benefit held for the Vietnam Moratorium Committee at Madison Square Garden. We were invited to perform along with Harry Belafonte, Richie Havens, Dave Brubeck, and Jimi Hendrix, among others. Reportedly twenty-one thousand people were there cheering and clapping. It was a good show.

The main topic at one of our tribal meetings concerned another proposed benefit. Bob Currie, the production stage manager, and Bill Orton, the business manager, acting as emissaries from the chief, asked whether the tribe would be willing to help raise money for the United Nations so that kids from all over the world could come to the U.N. for an International Youth Conference. According to the newspapers, Michael Butler had pledged at least $112,500 against a promise of raising $225,000. In the beginning, a big deal was made out of Michael Butler's concern over the plight of the American Indian. Early profits from *Hair* were supposedly given to the Tribal Peace Fund. Now the tune had changed to an anthem, supporting a United Nations program. Recalling how Michael Butler had put down society and the Establishment to the original Broadway cast, I couldn't get with this latest pledge. It almost seemed to me that he was trying to impress someone or even get involved in politics. It wasn't all that far-fetched. He had once run for the Illinois state senate in 1966 and lost. Six months after the tribal meeting about the U.N. Youth Conference, I was not surprised to read in an *Esquire** magazine profile:

MICHAEL BUTLER: "I admire achievement in any field, of any kind."

INTERVIEWER: " . . . even if it's success at evil?"

MICHAEL BUTLER: "Yes. It has nothing to do with contentment or moral judgment. I'm interested in power. I know who I am and where I'm at. My trip is a power trip."

INTERVIEWER: "When you bind people to you in this

*"A Weekend With Chief Michael Butler and His Inner Tribe," Helen Lawrenson, Nov. 1970

way, doesn't it destroy their own egos?" (He smiled faintly).

MICHAEL BUTLER: "They can always quit."

Then he went on to say: "I'm planning to go into politics in a heavy way . . . in a behind-the-scenes power role. I'm making plans now."

We had another tribal meeting over the U.N. benefit. It was to be my last one.

I have nothing against young people from all over the world having a conference at the U.N., but all around me I see people with more pressing, immediate needs—the people of Appalachia, the coal miners, the drug victims, those who live in urban ghettoes, not to mention the American Indian. I feel we should all help each other, but as my mother used to say, "Charity starts at home and spreads abroad." To me an International Youth Conference amounted to little more than a paid vacation. There's enough *talk* in the world as it is, not enough action.

Naturally I expressed my opinions loud and clear. While I was talking, Bill Orton and Bob Currie madly took notes. I didn't think it was because they dug what I was saying so much as wanting to get down *exactly* what I said for management. I knew my days were numbered, but it didn't stop me. I said I would help raise money for any cause that the entire cast agreed upon needed our help the most. But this just smelled of another publicity stunt for the show, another laurel for management's head. Many of the cast felt the way I did and said so, but in the long run they agreed to help raise the money under certain conditions: that they would do the show for the U.N. if they could also do it for Odyssey and Phoenix houses, and any other cause of their choice. They wound up doing the benefit. For me there had been too many deceits, too many broken promises. I knew better.

Shortly after my last tribal meeting, a person high in management warned me that I was going to be fired along with two others—George Tipton and Jonathan Kramer—because of our stands on the U.N. benefit. When I confronted Bill Orton with the rumor, he, of course, denied it.

In the midst of everything else, I was trying to get some time off to follow through on a few job leads. I spoke to Bill Orton about it one Friday. It was a repeat performance; he kept putting me off. He said they didn't have anyone else to do Abie or "White Boys." There was always some excuse.

"Are you going to give me time off?" I asked.

"No," Bill said.

"Then I'll have to leave."

"Come back on Monday. We'll discuss it."

47

Sunday was my birthday and I wanted to do something special. I decided to throw a party for myself at the home of a friend in Woodstock, New York.

The problem was who to invite. The best solution seemed to be to invite the entire cast of *Hair,* and everybody else connected with the show. There were some I didn't particularly want to come, but I invited everybody anyway.

When I invited Bill Orton, I jokingly told him that if everyone showed up we could stage a production of *Hair* in Woodstock. He told me that the *Hair* company had a small fund for parties, which, if I agreed, would pay for part of it. I agreed.

Preparation for the party went on for days. Thirteen chickens had been marinating in white wine since Thursday. With a few friends I arrived in Woodstock at six o'clock Sunday morning, and after putting away the food, we decided to crash for a few hours.

Our quarters turned out to be a cabin, surrounded by a waterfall and a beautiful lake. There was a small bridge on the way to the cabin, on which I stood for a moment. I couldn't believe it was real.

The place was just as beautiful in the daylight as it had been at dawn. Before every party I give, I go through pre-party paranoia: "What if nobody shows up? Maybe nobody's going to come?" In this case, considering the distance people had to travel, it seemed even justified.

At about three in the afternoon, people began to arrive by the carloads. Some of the kids from the *Hair* office were the first to arrive. Then a station wagon full of the cast pulled up. Bob Chapman made his entrance in a big, black limousine with a white chauffeur. The rest were friends and friends-of-friends outside of *Hair*.

The day was sunny. People dug the surroundings and hung out doing whatever they felt like doing. It was a far cry from Fire Island. Many freaked over the waterfall and lake; some played volleyball; others never left the barbecue pit. I supplied soda, beer and lots of food. Some people brought wine and pot. There was a radio playing inside the main house, but nobody was listening or dancing. Someone was playing the guitar outside.

As I had hoped, cast gripes and backstage bullshit were left behind at the Biltmore. All I wanted was for everyone to have a good time. I wasn't trying to recapture what we had with the original Broadway cast—I know nothing stays the same; that was gone forever—but still the party was special.

After dark, it started to drizzle, and we all went inside the main house. A few of the kids were high and started goofing; nobody seemed to want to leave. By the time the party finally started winding down, it was after midnight.

Emmeretta Marks and I stayed overnight, then drove

down in the morning. Monday, *Hair* and I parted company.

As he had requested, I went back to see Bill Orton, the business manager.

"Can I have time off for a leave of absence?"

"No."

"Then you give me no choice." It was a mutual agreement.

He offered me a release from *Hair*.

I should have left the show long before I did. I wasn't getting anything creative out of it anymore, and I was prepared to leave.

Although management had no reason to fire me, they wanted to get rid of me. They considered me a leader, which I was at that time, and a trouble-maker. I don't know about that. I do know I never stopped telling it like I saw it come down. I was never sure of my position in the show because I could never get with their games.

A guy in the cast told me that I was "a pivotal point in *Hair*. When the shit was flying you would always call everybody's attention to it," he said. "Most of us didn't want to hear it. We resented being told the truth, especially when it threatened the lies we'd built up so beautifully. In effect, they were trying to protect their lies against your truth, and that went on all the time, because there were so many lies going on."

I'd come full circle. I had closed that show too many times emotionally. It was just a matter of getting my body out of there.

I didn't do the show that Monday night, nor did I work the last two weeks. I went back to my dressing room to pick up my stuff. When I told the propmen I was leaving, they were shocked: "What's going to happen now?," they asked.

In the beginning of the show, if someone had told me that this was the way I would leave—just walking out with no fuss, no mess, no bother—I would have told them they were nuts. Even when things began to fall apart I never thought I'd be happy not doing *Hair*. The cast could have cared less about my leaving. It meant more for them to do onstage. Since I had virtually created the part of Abie, I felt nobody could do it like I could, but after I left, management brought in a girl who had played Abie in the Chicago *Hair* to replace me.

Next to Sally Eaton, I was the last of the original Broadway cast to leave the show. She was the only original "tribe member" left.

Right before leaving, I had heard a rumor that Ted Rado, Jim Rado's brother, was coming in from California to redirect the New York *Hair,* and that he didn't want to work with *any* of the original Broadway cast. It sounded to me like management wanted to start all over again with kids who were as fresh and innocent as we were in the beginning, kids who weren't hip to their tricks. It was no longer my concern.

I was never so glad to leave anything in my whole life.

48

When I got an invitiation to *Hair*'s third annual birthday celebration, I couldn't believe where it was going to take place: The Cathedral Church of St. John the Divine.

It figured. Last year profanity (semi-nudity); this year piety. The way I was brought up, there was a distinct difference between the secular and the sacred. Obviously the *Hair* powers-that-be were interested in an even higher Judgment. It had to be the publicity coup of the year.

The feature was a "Mass in F" composed and conducted by Galt MacDermot and performed by the cast of *Hair* with the cathedral choir. I already loved Galt's secular music; I could not imagine it ecclesiastic.

Originally, Galt wrote the "Mass" for the church he and his family attend in Staten Island. When *Hair* management heard about it . . . I decided to go, more to hear it than for any other reason.

Erroll Addison Booker, Bob Chapman, George Tipton and I—all *Hair* veterans now—drove to the church together in George's car. On the way we were all reminiscing and joking about having been in the show together.

With the exception of Lamont's death and some of the Phantom's sicker pranks, everything seemed hilarious in retrospect. We had all been there and back again. It was almost like belonging to a very exclusive club. Even though my taste in churches runs to something smaller and more intimate, I couldn't help being impressed with St. John's. *Hair* always did do everything in a big way. As we entered the cathedral, balloons imprinted with "God Is Love" floated all around us.

We couldn't find seats, so Galt told us to sit with the *Hair* cast. Inside, St. John's was more awesome than outside. Everything—Galt, the band, choirs, electronic recording, and televising equipment—was set up in and around the altar. I just could not get into it. It was clear how *Hair* was using the church, but I couldn't see what the church was getting out of it.

Looking around, I spotted Sally Eaton, who was still with the show. She looked like she had just stepped out of a Joan Crawford movie, which was not her usual look: high-heels, a midi-dress, a pillbox hat with a veil. When she took off her gloves, I noticed her nails were manicured.

Then the organist started playing "Aquarius" and I got goose bumps. Except for the cathedral acoustics, the band sounded as great as always, especially with Galt conducting. Songs from *Hair* were interspersed throughout the mass, which consisted of five numbers—Kyrie, Gloria, Sanctus, Benedictus, and The Lord's Prayer. People had been turning gospel music into Pop Rock for years. I wondered how the white people would like The Lord's Prayer rescored as rock.

There seemed to be an actual mass going on throughout the whole recital. The audience-congregation solemnly knelt to receive communion. The priest blessed and gave out the sacrament. People lifted their heads to receive the Holy Eucharist; then bowed reverently. Except for the TV cameraman, who was busily shooting the whole ritual over the priest's shoulder, it was just an ordinary act of beseeching God's grace. Michael Butler was one of those receiving communion.

Along with the usual sermon, speakers stood up to laud *Hair* and its far-reaching influence: how good it was; how much it had done for society; how it had awakened people to their wrongdoings, to *hypocrisy*. One of the speakers was Dr. Harvey Cox of the Harvard Divinity School.

Every time someone made a *Hair*-Is-Holy statement, the entire *Hair* cast, past and present, would groan and shake their heads: "If you only knew...." "Are you kidding?"

Michael Butler sat there basking in the praise.

CURTAIN CALL I

The phone was ringing.

"Happy Birthday!" cried Fred Rheinglas, now artistic director and production manager of *Hair*.

"Happy birthday for what?"

"It's the fourth anniversary of *Hair*." So it was—April 29, 1972. Michael Butler was giving a party for the cast at Butler's, his health food store and restaurant. Would I like to go with Fred?

"Yep." After all this time I was curious to see the changes, if any. But now I considered it a research project.

Fred told me to meet him at the Biltmore Theater later on that evening. On my way, while crossing 48th Street, I bumped into Jim Rado.

Two months before, I had thrown a get-together at my apartment. A few of the kids—lost "members of the tribe"—wanted to go check out *Hair*, mostly as a goof. But we couldn't get into watching it, it was so bad, and wound up talking to Gerry and Jim backstage. Gerry was playing Berger for Sunday performances mostly. He looked like an old man compared to all the kids. He had gotten heavier and aged, or at least looked closer to his real age, somewhere in his late thirties, early forties. You could tell he was the oldest person onstage, but he still managed to get away with it, at least more than Jim.

Jim wasn't back in the show yet, although he'd said he planned to be.

"If Jim is going to do the show, I'm not going to do it the night he does," Gerry kept saying.

Jim had taken off his wig and looked even older than Gerry. The first time I saw him without it, I didn't know who he was. The top of his head was totally bald. The rest of his grayish-blond hair fell to his shoulders.

"You and Gerry are supposed to be good actors," I said. "Why do you keep hanging on to *Hair*? Why don't you go and do something else?"

"Nobody offered anything," Jim said.

Nobody has to offer you anything, I was thinking. You should go out and get it. Someone once said that Gerry and Jim had a maternal attitude toward *Hair,* as though they were sheltering a child. Now it was like they were in their dotage.

When I spotted Jim on the street I goofed on not recognizing him at first, then we walked to the Biltmore together.

The photographs in the display cases outside the Biltmore contained shots of all the *Hair* companies on one side and glossies of the kids in the present Broadway cast on the other. Many of the faces were familiar, but one in particular stood out. Shelly Plimpton was back in the show. She must have been in and out of *Hair* more than any other cast member anywhere. I guess it paid the rent.

Inside the theater, the band was really cooking. I

didn't even have to look: I could hear Jimmy Lewis on bass, Idris Muhammad on drums, and Galt, who was conducting that night, on electric piano. I missed Steve Gillette on guitar. No matter what, the music was still very together, especially when Galt was there.

As I sat down to watch the show, I felt as though I had never had any connection with it at all. Staring at the stage, thoughts about Lamont Washington and what had happened began to explode in my head. Fragments of twenty-five months lit on and off like fireflies in the darkness. The feeling of feeling nothing is very strange.

I was sitting in the orchestra, which was little more than three-quarters full. The balcony had even fewer people. If a show can't sell out on a Saturday night, it's going out.

The kids onstage acted like suburban hippies on a weekend bender in the East Village. They reminded me of the *Hair* groupies, except that most of them looked like copies of the original and early post-original Broadway cast. The guy playing Berger was a double for Allan Nicholls, who'd replaced Barry McGuire. One girl was a carbon of Suzannah Norstrand; another of Natalie Mosco; another, Melba. There was a boy who didn't look like Ronnie Dyson but had other similar qualities in manner.

Obviously they were still casting from the original molds, but when it came to talent all resemblances stopped. People who had been doing bit parts in the chorus, badly, and who had left, were back performing lead roles.

I know every production can't be the same, and I didn't want to make comparisons or criticize the show particularly, but I could not help myself.

While I was still in *Hair*, I saw *Man Of La Mancha*

for the first time in a road company production in Boston. Watching it I thought, "This is great." I told my boyfriend how I felt.

"This is awful," he replied. "You should have seen it on Broadway with Richard Kiley, Irving Jacobson, and Joan Diener. This is all right, but it doesn't compare with the original."

Suddenly I realized that for people who had no basis for comparison, what they saw of any production is what they got. Since I was a part of the creation of the Broadway *Hair*, I couldn't help but read my feelings into an audience which was seeing something less than the original production. For first nighters, *Hair* might still have been everything they had heard it would be. For me, it was like watching an old man who was even past trying to recapture his youth. There was no life in it at all.

Gerry Ragni and friends happened to be sitting next to me. "Oh, Mary Davis did this better and that better," I heard him jive. He was teasing, but all through it I thought he was so blind that he couldn't, or wouldn't see what had happened to his show.

"They should hire actors," I thought. "The whole hippie-love epoch is dead and they should hire professionals."

When *Hair* started to fall apart, so did the *Hair* groupies' fascination with it. At the age of sixteen Dennis Erdman had told me: "The show's losing its pure quality, because of the phony people in it. It bothers me to see people ruining it."

At eighteen, Dennis summed up *Hair*'s decline another way: "It isn't a question of growing up, it's just a question of changing your values. The age of Aquarius, the age of falling out and freaking out, is over. *Hair* swept through the country and glorified this type of attitude. It was like a freak revolution. It no longer mattered what you were like inside, it mattered what you *looked* like.

"*Hair* contributed to the drug culture, because more and more people started to join the freak revolution and lost their identity essentially during that. I just wanted to be in *Hair*. . . . I didn't know anything about voice, anything about acting, or anything."

That's what was being reflected up on that stage.

I couldn't stand sitting there anymore. I went backstage to find Fred, but he was upstairs so I wandered around backstage. I didn't want to see anyone heavy from management and have to go through changes about how great the show still is, "isn't it?" I knew I would tell them what I really thought.

The propmen were sitting around a prop table looking exactly the same: like it was the day before payday. "You're just doing the job," I thought. We exchanged a few words, I ran into the electrician. I saw the stage manager calling his cues. Everybody was just doing his job. The kids onstage were going through all the motions of the "Woodstock Nation" incarnate, but backstage no one even bothered to pretend.

The stage manager told me that Fred was with Tom O'Horgan, who had just returned from Egypt. I went back out to sit with the audience and wait out the rest of the show. It was almost like punishment.

Finally, the finale.

"Let The Sunshine In" is, or should be, the high point of the show. Most of the cast were screaming the song in a throat-ruining pitch, as though volume could make up for content. When they started walking to the foot of the stage, some inched their way in front of others, shoulders first, then the rest of their bodies. That got me.

"Look at them, just look at them," I nudged Gerry. "You can see them doing it." Everything else may go through changes, but upstaging always remains the same. Seeing it again brought it all back.

The cast was bringing people up onstage. Jim Rado, who was sitting behind me, tapped me on the shoulder. "Come on, Mary, let's go up."

The kids onstage who knew me said hello. I joined in the singing. Tom O'Horgan was standing in the wings. His hair was a good two or three inches below his shoulders, and he was dressed in some kind of near-Eastern shirt. He looked terrific. He was smiling and letting it all happen. He also seemed to be taking mental notes. When he saw me, he came onstage and gave me a big bear hug. It was the first real up of the evening.

Butler's is situated in a brownstone on East 60th Street. Anticipating another evening of carrots, brown rice, and sunflower seeds, I had already eaten. There was a buffet spread on the downstairs patio, and the whole scene had a studied "let's-have-a-party-in-the-garden" effect.

A lot of the kids from the present cast were there. Some said they had never even met Michael Butler; some admitted they didn't even know who he was.

Upstairs, the first person I saw as I walked through the door was the Great White Hope himself. Tanned and dressed all in white, Michael Butler stood out conspicuously, towering over everyone else. He looked handsome, handsome and uptight. To me he always looked uptight, even from the first time we had met at Variety Arts.

Michael Butler was supposed to be greatly influenced by Genghis Khan, the Mongolian conqueror, who—with his nine administrators—managed to conquer most of Asia in the Thirteenth Century. By April 1972, Michael Butler and his "administrators" (called the "clan") managed to "conquer" more than twenty-six million theatergoers in twenty-two countries throughout the world. *Hair* had been performed in fourteen languages.

Nevertheless, Michael Butler looked alone and insecure to me. I know he saw me, but I ignored him at first. He was surrounded by people, as usual, and I wanted to talk to him but not until the right moment.

The party was a rerun of all the other *Hair* parties I had ever been to. I never could get into them. Most of the representatives from the *Hair* confederacy who were at the party looked very prosperous and seemed satisfied with themselves. They had made a bundle from the show, and nobody was more impressed by it than they were. Galt and his wife were there. I was glad to see them.

Finally, it was time to talk to the great man himself. I approached him through a rift in the wall of people around him.

"How are you?" I said with my hand out to shake his, but he put his arm around me instead, hugging me and saying, "Mary, how are you?"

"Fine. You look fabulous," I told him, meaning it. I don't think Michael Butler ever knew what I was going to say or do next. I dug talking to him especially for that reason. But I wasn't bullshitting him. He did look great.

"It's good to see someone from the old company," he said. "You're the only one from the original cast that came to see the show today."

We both knew that if it hadn't been for Fred I never would have been there. I didn't get an invitation nor, judging from their absence, did any of the other members of the original cast. Management knew my address: for my past three birthdays the *Hair* company had sent me a present of a small, gold-like charm with astrological and metaphysical symbols embossed on both sides. The only ones recognizable to me were Sagittarius (Michael Butler's birth sign), Aquarius (*Hair*'s elected birth sign), and the symbol of infinity.

Finally, he said, "Happy birthday, Mary."

"Not happy birthday to me," I said. "Happy birthday to *you*."

I suddenly felt sorry for him. He should have been much more together than I thought he was.

We parted. As I walked away from him some guy with a familiar face bumped into me roughly and then headed for Michael Butler. It was Mick Jagger. Everyone did a whole number on them. Eventually they walked out the front door together and left the party.

Happy birthday, *Hair*.

CURTAIN CALL II

In early May, soon after the party at Michael Butler's, I got an invitation (in the form of a small Frisbee) to attend an international *Hair* concert in Central Park's Mall.

It was hard to believe there still was a *Hair*. The *Daily News* called the event "joyous." The whole thing looked to me like one of those unrehearsed benefits we used to do, with everybody outscreaming and upstaging everybody else. They were trying. What *Hair* had to say wasn't all over, but evidently *Hair* was.

On July 1, 1972, after 1,742 performances on Broadway and ". . . a profit of about $6,286,565 from all sources on a $150,000 capitalization,"* *Hair* finally closed. I did not go, but I was told that the last show, like the first, had been a complete sell-out. People lined up for hours outside the Biltmore. Every performer present who had ever played *Hair* was invited to join in the big numbers.

By the finale, the cast had tripled in size. Everyone was crying and carrying on. Hundreds from the audience

*Variety, July 5, 1972

rushed the stage during curtain call. Gerry wasn't there, but Jim wandered around onstage shaken and grief-stricken. Hoards of people waited for the performers, outside the theater like *Hair* groupies.

The Age of Aquarius was officially over.

Hair was different from other shows because what was happening onstage was happening at that particular moment on the streets. By the time the New York version closed, the show had been seen all over the United States—in Los Angeles, San Francisco, Chicago, Boston, Las Vegas, Seattle, Miami, Detroit, St. Paul, Evansville, Des Moines, Indianapolis, Phoenix, Kansas City (Kansas), Cincinnati. Abroad it had appeared in London, Paris, Sao Paolo, Munich, Helsinki, Belgrade, Sydney, Amsterdam, Tokyo, Stockholm, Copenhagen, Tel Aviv, and Athens. Rough estimates have put the total receipts at over seventy-three million dollars.

After talking with just about everyone in the Broadway company, I've never heard anyone say they didn't like doing the show. Performances always felt good because most of the original cast believed in what they were saying, and that's unusual for a show. We were conditioned in our exercises with Tom O'Horgan to believe in what we were doing; we got caught up in the music and the general feeling of freedom while onstage, which was a true moment in life, a high in itself. That's the reason most people didn't just quit when the offstage hassles flared up. Everyone wanted to stay onstage. Some people stayed because they were being paid to do something they enjoyed doing, and—let's face it—we all got a lot of prestige from being in the original Broadway company. And still do. *Hair* had an amazing effect on a lot of people (many of them now in the Establishment). It was more than a play: it tried to sell a message to the world. Maybe that was the big mistake. If they hadn't sold a dream—and if we hadn't bought it—maybe things would have been cooler, the way they are in any show. But it wasn't billed that way to us—or to the public. *Hair* sold its message offstage as well as on—that was part of the package.

After we opened, I think one reason cast members showed up late or stayed out was to get some relief from the management's bullshit, and also because they were led to believe they could get away with it. If someone tells you rules are made to be broken, why obey them? The show started deteriorating when the performers started realizing they were not a "love tribe," just a bunch of actors for hire. You could summarize our feeling by saying that in the beginning we felt like newborn children but in the end we were more like terminal cases.

The deterioration started when cast members began caring less about the show and more about the benefits. Cast members were late, absent, high, undisciplined, careless on stage, and generally obnoxious at the theater. So the show became a mess. The last time I saw *Hair* I was embarrassed for the people onstage because they were bad, and I was bored and sorry the show had come to this.

But the deterioration didn't end there. It seems as if almost everyone in the original Broadway show, and some who followed, had some sort of emotional problem when they left *Hair* and had to pull themselves together.

Several of the original cast, and a few who came later, had nervous breakdowns. Three guys were heavily into drugs and psychotherapy by the time they and *Hair* parted company. One of them is off drugs now, at least the hard stuff. Another, who was on drugs, is now off but acts as a guinea pig for experiments by a large drug house to earn extra money. Another o.d.-ed in Chicago but managed to pull through.

In fact, Jonathan Kramer told me that he had to leave the country to get himself together. After *Hair* he went to London to do "The Dirtiest Show in Town," then returned to the States to do a road tour of "Jesus Christ Superstar," and, last I heard, he had gone back to England.

Paul Jabara also went to England. The New York *Times* reported that he had chained himself to the prime minister's gate overnight because they wouldn't give him a work permit to perform in a show. He never got it, either. He also has been working on his own musical and has written a show that's supposed to be produced on Broadway.

It seems like a few of the kids from the original cast will never get it back together again. I heard that one of the girls is a junkie who works as a hooker to support her habit. She tried methadone and might be off the streets now; I don't know.

I was told that another girl entered Bellevue Hospital suffering from malnutrition. After *Hair,* she eventually moved from her uptown luxury highrise apartment back to a tenement on the Lower East Side. I know she used to be heavily into drugs.

One girl in the cast who was going with one guy had another guy's baby, and from what I hear, tried to kill herself a few times.

Someone told me that another girl, who's a success now, is going to a shrink. I'm told that she's really changed, that she's fooling around with drugs a lot, heavy stuff, and that she freaks out occasionally.

But while *Hair* hurt a lot of people, it helped others, too. One member of the original cast did a complete about-face after leaving *Hair*. Walter Harris always had trouble with his leg in the show, and after it closed I heard from his father that he'd had a leg amputated. But in spite of that, Walter was studying to become a Jesuit priest.

Some of the kids from the original Broadway cast moved into other phases of show biz. When Erroll Addison Booker left *Hair* he got heavily into skag (heroin) and a bad scene in general. Someone accidentally shot him in the knee and now he walks with a limp. But he is completely off the stuff, and, last I heard, is studying at a university in upstate New York, specializing in the management side of the theater.

Many of the kids are still working in the theater or clubs or making records. Ronnie Dyson has a couple of record albums, including the hit singles, "Why Can't I Touch You" and "One Man Band." I heard Lynn Kellogg was living on a farm in California and occasionally performs in night clubs and on TV. Sally Eaton does singing dates in small clubs around New York.

Leata Galloway has performed in some Off-Broadway shows and is doing stuff for Cafe La MaMa. Robert I. Rubinsky is writing a film, "Yentas On the Cosmos."

Still others from the cast have continued their careers as performers. I have. Donnie Burks played in Broadway's *Two Gentlemen of Verona* for which Galt MacDermot wrote the music.

For a while I was worried that Donnie would become a victim of what I called the Hud Hex. Everyone who played the part died under tragic circumstances. Lamont.

Then Jim Fields got the part. When he was fired from the New York company, he went to Australia where he played Hud Down Under. Then, on a trip to Europe, the Hud Hex struck again. Jim was killed falling off a mountain. When Jim left, Donnie took over the part. I was understudy for Hud and I know. I got strange vibes just thinking about it.

Two of the original cast, Melba Moore and Diane Keaton, are well-known now. Melba received a Tony Award for her performance in *Purlie* and does nightclub and TV gigs. Diane received a Tony nomination for *Play It Again, Sam.* She also played in the movie *The Godfather.*

Hiram Keller also went on to bigger and better things as co-star in Fellini's *Satyricon.* He is still doing movies in Europe and hanging out with the jet-set.

Some of the original cast seemed to have dropped completely out of sight. The last time I saw Margi LiPari she was writing her own music and getting it together for club and record work. Natalie Mosco, who's been living in Australia, wrote me that she plans to return to the U.S. soon. The last I heard from Emmeretta Marks, she looked fabulous and was living in the Plaza Hotel with some guy. She also appeared in the movie *The Groupies* and sang in *Scarecrow in a Garden of Cucumbers.*

Although he was not in the original Broadway cast, Ben Vereen is now a big star. He was nominated for a Tony for *Superstar* in 1972 and won a Tony in 1973 for his role in *Pippin,* as did Jules Fisher, who designed the show's lighting.

Michael Butler, from all reports, is still involved in *Hair.* There are periodic notices that he plans to make it into a film. Some of the tribe members have got together again.

Gerry Ragni and Galt wrote the musical *Dude,* which was quickly dubbed "Dud" by the media when it flopped to the tune of approximately $900,000. When I saw the first preview I was embarrassed for everyone involved, although I thought some of Galt's music was just as good as the music from *Hair.*

Another Broadway musical disaster of similar magnitude was *Via Galactica.* Galt wrote the score for this one, and it was not his best. Even though I was in the show, I still don't understand what they were trying to do.

Dude lasted two weeks, *Via Galactica,* one; but *Rainbow,* Jim and Ted Rado's musical, outlived them both. As I watched *Rainbow,* I saw faces of people who had been involved in one or another of the numerous *Hair* companies, both in the cast and on the production staff. None were from the original Broadway company, however. The costumes were created by *Hair* costumer Nancy Potts. Clive Barnes said in his review of *Rainbow* that it ". . . almost literally takes off from where *Hair* ended." It would have been better if it had picked up from where *Hair* began.